HEADS OR TAILS

HEADS OR TAILS

A Physician's Journey from Doctor to Patient

JOSEPH VARUGHESE, M.D.

Published by Elizabeth Varughese
jvheadsortails@gmail.com
ISBN: 978-0-615-87538-5

Library of Congress Control Number: 2011916010

Cover and book design by Michele de la Menardiere
Edited by Dan McNeill

Front cover photos: Joseph Varughese © Eduardo Montoya; Twin Palm © Sunil
Menon; Young man in water © ALIJA.
Back cover photo: Joseph Varughese © Madhu John, M.D.

Dedication

To my parents
M.P. Varughese and Thankamma Varughese

APPACHEN
Who taught me faith, integrity and perseverance

and

AMMACHY
Whose loving spirit is my guiding force

CONTENTS

PART I

HEADS

CHAPTER 1

The Coin

From Easter Island to Siberia, people know the metaphor of heads-or-tails. And most cultures consider heads the winner and tails the loser — or is it the other way around? Let's say heads is the more fortunate side and tails is the less. My life has been like a coin which has flipped many times and it continues to flip even as I pen my thoughts.

I grew up deep in the Third World. My small village had no electricity till I was 10, and imaginary forces in the black night terrified me as a child. I never saw running water till I was 13 or television till 26, and I learned typing and computer use at 35. The village had no hospital or medical care, and an experienced local mother delivered me as a baby, cutting my umbilical cord with a kitchen knife boiled in water. Forty years later I had a leading-edge medical practice in the huge, glittering metropolis of Los Angeles. Who flipped the coin?

I often hear the question, "Where did you come from originally?" Patients, colleagues, neighbors, grocery store clerks, and individuals from many other walks of life ask me this question, and my answer differs depending on the person's culture, vocation, and ethnicity.

Usually, I just say, "India," and this response satisfies them. The more curious ask, "Which part of India?" I tell them that I am from Kerala, a state in southern India. Kerala is known as the "land of coconut trees."

People worldwide have seen tourist pictures of its rice fields and beaches studded with palm trees, their trunks swooping out over the tropical sea.

I grew up inland, in the village called Mallapally, whose name derived from *mallan*, meaning "strong people," and *pally*, or "place." According to legend, the local maharaja visited Mallapally and the citizens brought out an elephant to greet him, clutching the animal tightly so it wouldn't escape and hurt him. Much impressed, the ruler declared that a village with so many powerful residents deserved the name "place of strongmen," or Mallapally.

I first became interested in medicine when I was six. My mother had been feeling extreme fatigue and had swelling in her legs. The only treatment available was from the local healer, who had tended our family for many years: Baby Vydhyan. ("Baby" is a common name in Kerala and "*vydhyan*" means medicine man.) He was in his 50s, small-boned and soft-spoken. On most days he wore no shirt but rather a shawl-like cloth around his neck.

Baby Vydhyan saw my mother's condition and sent us out to collect leeches from the paddy field. They looked like thick black threads when we picked them up and brought them in. He applied two or three to each leg. "Keep an eye on them," he said, "and don't scratch or rub the area."

After a few hours of drinking my mother's blood, the leeches had swollen to the size of baby carrots and lolled sluggishly from side to side, but still clung to her skin. Baby Vydhyan ordered a calcium carbonate liquid prepared by crushing the shells of garden snails in salt water. He poured it over the leeches and one by one they released their grip and dropped. My mother felt no different and her legs remained swollen.

The *vydhyan* instructed our servant lady to give her "sweat therapy" the following day. (The literal translation is: "We will sweat out the fluid.") Mother lay on a small rope cot, with a thin mattress beneath her and blankets on top. The servant brought a pot of boiling water and put it beneath her bed. The steam rose up through the ropes and mattress, but the blankets trapped it as in a sauna and I saw perspiration pouring from my mother's forehead. This ordeal continued for an hour. When the pot cooled, more hot water arrived. The medicine man sat on a chair at the end of the veranda and occasionally felt her pulse and asked how she was doing. These treatments continued for about a week. In the end, my mother felt better and her swelling went down. She was always grateful to him and respected him a great deal.

Everything looked magical to me at that age and the medicine man's actions were compelling drama. I grew curious about his knowledge of fluid overload and his methods of reducing it. The esteem and grateful glances he received from his patients also had an impact on me.

Looking back, I think my mother had congestive cardiac failure. She had had a heart attack about four years before, when she was 42. And even though we have much better treatment these days, I learned that one can practice medicine and relieve suffering in many ways. Later we moved to a bigger town, Tiruvalla, where Mother received proper medical care and was able to lead a normal life. She lived to the age of 82 and died in her sleep.

Tiruvalla had hospitals and modern medicine. When my mother took me to the doctor for a cold or a fever, I was spellbound. I absorbed every little detail. After the doctor examined me, he would give my mother a slip of paper and we would visit the pharmacy. I saw hundreds of bottles sitting on the shelves, and felt astonishment and even awe at how the doctor could figure out which one was right for me.

Curiosity is a driving force in my life and it guided my choice of a career as a physician. This dream was not easy to attain and would take years and years of hard work. But I paid little attention to the obstacles. My parents understood my drive and supported me in realizing my vision.

Decades later, I had gone from a life in a developing country to one in a land on the other side of the world that offered immense opportunity and freedom to the people lucky enough to be born there. My life was rich and rewarding, and I imagined I would live happily ever after in the United States.

Then the coin flipped again. From seeing leeches suck blood out of the body, I would watch mesmerized as stem cells flowed into my veins. From the most ancient form of medicine, I would be catapulted into the most advanced treatments on earth. From being a doctor, I would become a patient.

Life challenges you with surprises beyond your imagination. Things feel fine and proper when we are on the fortunate side, but when the coin flips the whole world changes and the good times suddenly seem far away. And the laws of nature allow many different paths in our lives. Some people are fated to have more flips than others.

Why is life such an easy ride for some and a bumpy one for others? Why do some have everything at birth while others struggle to meet their needs? Why do some couples enjoy happy marriages while others wonder what happiness even is? Why are some born with disabilities while others never have to think about their health? Why are some brilliant while others need hours and hours of studying to learn? Why are some born in affluent countries and others in poverty-stricken ones? I have grappled with these questions and continue to wonder: Who flips the coin that decides your lot in life?

CHAPTER 2

Grandmother and Ghosts

The family dynamics in my childhood were not normal.

Before my birth, my father M.P. Varughese had worked in Bombay for the McKinnon and McKenzie Company. In 1945 it began recruiting educated people who could type and write letters to work in their Persian Gulf branches for a slightly higher salary. Since he had a B.A. degree, he qualified and left India for Basra, in Iraq. World War II was still going on, and he later told us stories about the British naval ships escorting cargo and passenger ships to the Gulf coast to avoid mines and prevent submarine attacks.

He took this risk since his responsibilities were more pressing than his perils from the journey. My parents then had four other children — two brothers in boarding school and two sisters — and later there was me and my younger sister Molly. My father had to make enough money to give my older sisters a dowry and pay the tuition for my older brothers. Mother had to go with him, since there were no hotels or friends in those days for cooking and running a house.

By the time I was born in 1949, he was working in Muscat, the capital of Oman, where he spent the rest of his career. I lived there until the age of five, when my parents sent me to live with Grandmother back in Mallapally. My father could not afford to have me educated in an expensive

European school and the local school taught only in Arabic. My parents decided I would attend school in Kerala.

Grandmother was a thin woman with silvery hair and long earlobes like the females' in certain African tribes, as she used to wear heavy earrings in her younger days. She had a shrill voice and a commanding personality. She made her presence known and was not afraid of demanding services or confronting people who disagreed with her. Since she had been widowed at a young age, everyone in the family accepted these traits as survival skills needed to run a house without a man. Father supported her and she had enough land to cultivate crops and manage a household. She enjoyed her independence and power over everything around her.

My arrival at her home was probably not in her life plan. She was used to living as she pleased, and now she had to accommodate to my needs, from schooling to meals. Since the family and society accepted this arrangement as normal, she was forced to assume responsibility for her grandson. But I moved things and didn't put them back, which she did not like at all. I made noises and whistled, which annoyed her. I ran around the neighborhood and came home with dirty clothes, which created extra work for her. I climbed the coffee, guava, and mango trees, which irritated her, not because of the danger to me, but her fear that I might harm the tree or its ripening fruit. I missed my mother's love and longed to receive it from someone, but it would not be from my grandmother.

My aunt Mariamma was my safety net during all the years I lived with Grandmother. She had become a widow at 26, when she joined us in the household. She was gentle, compassionate, and affectionate — the opposite of Grandmother. She was attentive to all my daily needs such as bathing, eating, and sleeping. She compensated for Grandmother's harshness with her caring words and actions.

I rarely saw my parents. Father's contract paid for vacations only once every three years. My mother usually came in between for major family matters like my sisters' marriages, schooling for children, or her own mother's illness. I don't remember counting down the days on the calendar for my parents to be with me on their vacation, but their departures were always devastating and painful.

We had only one lamp in our house after sunset, when I lived with Grandmother, and we usually kept it in the kitchen as the servant needed to get dinner ready. The dining room was next to the kitchen, so the light from the kitchen was enough for me to sit and watch the cooking in progress. Grandmother forbade any other lamp in the house because of the high cost of kerosene. She constantly reminded us to use light frugally.

Psalm 119:105 says, "Your word is a lamp unto my feet and a light unto my path." Unless I held that lamp while walking, I had nothing to light my path. The whole night world was utterly dark and only the lamp showed the way for your footsteps. Living in Los Angeles, my kids have trouble appreciating the easy availability of electricity. I try hard to convey to them the luxury of getting light at the flick of a switch.

After dinner we had our family prayer and Grandmother lit another lamp for herself and went to bed. I slept on the floor, on a coconut fiber mat with a small pillow. I had no say in when she turned the lamp off. She countered all my requests for light with the kerosene argument.

Most of the floor in our house was dried mud. Two or three times a year, Grandmother smeared it with a liquid concoction of cow dung and leaves to make it crack-proof and waterproof. The fireplace was also built with mud on a raised platform. For fuel, we used dried leaves and dried branches picked from our backyard, as well as the plentiful coconut shells. The ashes needed cleaning every day before retiring.

On many nights, I slipped back into the kitchen to watch the servant lady Ammini wash the plates, listen to her stories, and ask lots of questions that crossed my mind. My aunt Mariamma, or "Peediyamalayil Ammachy," often joined us. Her stories bothered me because she would talk about ghosts and dark forces. Peering out into the blackness broken only by a light from the neighbor's house, she would tell me that the neighbor who died suddenly two weeks ago had been stricken by an evil spirit, and slap her thigh for emphasis. That sound would startle me and make my heart start thudding. I had the same feeling several times at night when I'd wake up to the noise of wind or the lonely bark of our watchdog. I longed for my mother, who would surely have hugged me tight, held me to her chest, reassured me that these were only myths, and waited till l fell asleep. Instead, I pulled my sheet over my head and shivered, listening to my heavy heartbeats until I dropped asleep from exhaustion.

As a child, these stories took a terrible toll on me. The world of darkness after sunset filled me with terror, and if I woke at night and had to go the bathroom it was a nightmare. We had no actual bathroom, though we had much acreage and we could use any convenient place for this purpose. In the middle of the night all I had to do was to step out of the house, but I could never find the courage to enter that great darkness alone. Luckily, Ammini and my aunt understood my fears and would accompany me.

Once I saw the funeral of a 16-year-old boy who drowned in the river and I listened to all the stories about him. The fear of death now haunted me. At night, I began hearing noises and sounds that I imagined were visits from the death angel or a ghost passing through the neighborhood. Since there was no electricity and the world around me was utterly black, I dreaded closing my eyes and falling asleep.

I had many questions for my aunt, but her answers reinforced my fear that ghosts stalked the neighborhood. Every time a dog howled, she said that the animal sensed things people could not and someone in the neighborhood was about to die. As a helpless child, that was not what I needed to hear. I had no one to reassure me and explain that these ideas were myths. Every night, I covered my head with my sheet so I would not hear any sounds.

In my sleep one night, a few days after my mother had left to join Father in Oman, I started screaming, "Ammachy (Mother)!" Our servant Ammini woke me from my nightmare and reassured me that I had been dreaming and missing my mother. She told me that, before she left, Mother came to my bedside while I was sleeping, kissed me several times, and promised she would return soon. Ammini explained that I was left behind because I had to go to school and start learning.

I vividly remember the family prayer before Mother left, as I clung to her under her sari with my face touching her bare midriff and soaking in her scent as much as I could. Ammini distracted me by taking me elsewhere in the neighborhood so I wouldn't see her actual departure. She would sing songs and tell stories, but a sense of heaviness, uncertainty, and insecurity consumed my mind and nothing could replace it.

Elementary school was probably my best distraction, but it occupied just a fraction of the day. The building was about a mile away from home. For the first few days after I began, one of our servants took me to school and later, some neighbors walked with me. But eventually the time came when I was on my own and had to cover that distance by myself. There were rumors that criminals kidnapped children from the villages and took them to cities, where they blinded them and used them for begging on the sidewalks. Their sightlessness generated sympathy in passers-by and more income for the kidnappers. The images of maimed children begging in the markets and streets filled my six-year-old mind.

Such fears consumed me as I walked alone to school. The road was very lonely and isolated. Occasionally, you saw a worker with an ax on his shoulder going to cut firewood for neighbors. On a lucky day, a bullock cart would come by and I'd follow along, listening to the wheels clicking and rumbling along the ruts of the rough road. But usually I was alone, and my senses were hyper-vigilant. I intermittently walked and ran until I reached school and the crowd and noise made me forget the distance I had covered with so much anxiety.

Once in school, the routine kept me going and I remember being happy there. The school was a shed with a thatched roof, and the classrooms were separated by waist-high walls made of matted coconut palms. We had a blackboard and chalk placed in a wooden box, and nothing else. There was no playground, but we had enough room around the school to play, climb trees, and dash about during recess.

Free lunch was the highlight of the day, facilitated by a grant from an international agency such as UNESCO. Each student had a small steel bowl filled with hot rice gruel and beans. I ate it like soup, using a cone-shaped spoon fashioned out of a jackfruit leaf.

The return from school was easier as the roads were more crowded and other kids in the neighborhood would walk me home if I asked. The journey back took more time as we scouted for mango trees with ripe fruits or picked up fallen cashew nuts. There were no school bags. All I had was a simple stone slate and a piece of soft graphite shaped like a pencil. I remember bringing home report cards on the slate where the teacher wrote my grades with a white chalk. Usually it read 100 out of 100.

But the happiness of such days faded into the fear of darkness, and the empty feeling of missing my parents filled my mind. With no electricity in the area, the world shrank to the flickering light of the lamps in the kitchen and dining area. I don't remember doing any homework at night, but my mind was always alert, listening to the sounds all around me. There was no music, but the crickets outside formed an orchestra in the dark. There were no radios for news, but the frogs in the neighborhood made enough noise to get your attention. There were no clocks, but the rooster never missed a morning wake-up call. There were no electric fans, but handheld ones made of coconut palms moved the air across my face on sultry nights. There were no bedtime tales, but the horror stories I heard during the day played out in my head.

There was also no heating or insulation for the house during the monsoon season when the thunderstorms kept me awake. Because I slept on the floor, I seemed to feel every raindrop that hit the earth. On some days the lightning flared so brightly that I thought the house would catch fire. The bed sheets were not warm enough to keep off the draft that swept through the house. There were no sympathetic ears to hear my concerns or fear, as rain and thunder were common there.

Eventually, at my request, Grandmother allowed a small lantern with the flames turned low to keep a glow in the room. On stormy nights, the draft put out the lantern and plunged my world into total darkness. I curled into a fetal position to keep warm and occasionally stretched my arms across the floor to touch Ammini's mat. I slept erratically and often I woke up several times wanting to feel my mother's shelter and warmth. But I was deprived of that protection and felt helpless.

In this atmosphere I developed a general sense of desperation with no means to express it. My mind fixated on horror stories and frightening events that happened nearby. A fear of darkness and death crept into my life at an early, vulnerable age and I have struggled with it all my life. Ironically, this baseless fear of death would become a very real one with my cancer diagnosis.

CHAPTER 3

The Betel Nut Chewer

In my emotional emptiness, a little seed was planted and started sprouting in me: that I was in this situation for one reason, to study. During the daytime I focused on my schoolwork, and learning became a driving force in my life. Wherever I was, I became passionate about studying new topics and developed a curiosity about many things.

Mallapally was famous for its number of college graduates. They were rare in those days, but my father was one of them and our family was very proud of him. As a child, I fervently wanted to become a physician, and education would be the road that led me from Mallapally to Southern California. But I faced many, many obstacles before I graduated from medical school.

My mind goes back to the time before I entered school, when I learned how to read and write. My first teacher was a man in his fifties. I had seen him around our neighborhood, often talking loudly in his husky voice. Everyone respected him and he was known as Avaran Sir. (Teachers enjoy great honor in our society and are called "Sir.") He liked to chew tobacco leaves and betel nuts, which colored his sputum bright red. His spitting caught people's attention, since a stream of blood seemed to be spurting from his mouth. He ignored me and I had never talked to him. His aura intimidated me.

When he appeared in my house one day and my parents announced that he was going to teach me the alphabet, my perspective changed. The fear disappeared and I developed a definite liking for this man who was going to unveil the mysteries of reading and writing.

We sat down on our veranda. He spread out rice grains on a table, put his index finger among them, and used it as a "pen" to write the first letter in the Malayalam alphabet. Then he had me do it, and asked me to speak out each character as I wrote. The method may seem crude, but the rice grains made nice patterns and the beauty of it is that you can easily write and erase the letters. My master was very keen that the letters should be big and round. The Malayalam script appeared around 830 A.D. and its name, *vatazhutu*, means "round letters." It has around 51 characters and I knew learning them would consume my days till I mastered them.

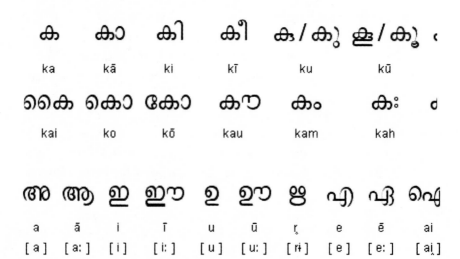

Vowel diacritics with ka

As the lessons progressed, the master had me make a permanent copy of each character on a special palm leaf, 3 by 9 inches. I etched the letter into the leaf using a pointed metal stylus, and then I could highlight it by rubbing it with a poppy seed-like plant to make it blue or with charcoal to make it black. When I finished all 51 letters, I had a stack of leaves with all the letters, and the master bound it on one corner by punching a hole with the stylus and stringing it with a thread. Looking back, that was my first graduation certificate. I wish I had kept it. Since then I lived in many houses, moved to three different continents and four different countries, and worked in fourteen different hospitals. It is only a memory for me now.

One thing I remember is my master telling my parents that I was a bright student and adding, "He will be someone some day." I never fretted about homework and in fact I always looked forward to the master arriving at my house so I could learn more.

Self-education has been a driving force in my life and I have been a lifelong student. I have passion for knowledge and I welcome change. I discovered very early that if we don't embrace change, we will be stuck in our past and present, and will miss our future.

I could have found excuses not to venture into anything new or broaden my skills. In fact, I have missed opportunities due to my lack of certain abilities. I didn't study in Lebanon because my conversational English wasn't up to par. I regret procrastinating and seeing opportunities slip away. For instance, I could have come to the United States 15 years earlier than I did.

Even so, destiny lifted me from a Third World village boy writing simple letters on palm leaves to a physician leading a major project to digitize medical records. I have seen some of my colleagues resist new technology and struggle with it, but I later convinced many of them that change is for our own good in the long term. The future more than repays us for the time and effort we spend learning new ways today.

CHAPTER 4

Rivers, Cashews, and Thorns

I lacked many talents and skills in my childhood, and I certainly missed many extracurricular activities like music and art that were available to my children. Yet growing up in a village had its advantages. Compared to smoggy Los Angeles, the air was pristine and the neighborhood was quiet.

My nephews and nieces were my cheerleaders back then. Since I was the youngest son in the family and my two older sisters seemed more like my mother, their children became my best friends. We grew up together and played together. Even today, my niece Leelamma tells stories about how I made her get chocolates from my father and pocketed them myself. Her sister Valsamma relates how we used to sing nursery songs forward and backward without missing the rhyme. My niece Annie describes how I taught her swimming but almost drowned in the canal. My nephew Prasad tells how he enjoyed riding behind me on a motorbike in the rugged terrain of his hometown and almost fell off because of my recklessness. I was technically their uncle, but we were really buddies.

From age five to ten, my whole world was within walking distance and my life followed a predictable routine.

Every family had its own well for clean water. In fact, we had two wells, one near our house and the other at the end of our property. The latter was close to a canal, so it was full throughout the year. The water was cold and clear, and we had plenty of it for domestic needs. You needed a strong back and a little balance to draw water from these wells, but it did not take much effort once you mastered the technique.

The canals and the nearby Manimala River were my preferred places for taking a bath. However, it was not just a bath, but half a day of activity. Half a day? Where did I find the time? Time seemed almost endless in my childhood days. We had no clock in our house. We woke up when the sun rose, around six am. When it was over our head we knew that it was lunchtime, and when the sun set at six pm it was time to retire.

So we used to swim up and down the stream, dive from rocks, and occasionally cross the river in a canoe. As in many villages, the river was for swimming, washing clothes, and simply gathering and chatting. It was a social center and people shared the neighborhood gossip during activities by the water.

In the rainy season, the river overflowed and for us it was the best time of the year. Everything lay submerged and there were no fences or boundaries to stop us, no sharp stones or uneven ground to trip over. We made rafts from banana stems pinned together by wooden sticks and floated around the whole area, going freely from yard to yard, responding to greetings from friends and neighbors peering through their windows.

My swimming teachers were my older brothers. There was not much in the way of instruction. They threw me in the river and lifted me up when I sank. The survival instinct was my main coach. Yet perhaps because I learned swimming early on, I have enjoyed aquatic activities all my life, including water skiing and snorkeling. I had my most memorable snorkeling experience at the Great Barrier Reef in Australia.

I don't remember having any manufactured toys in my childhood, but I did not miss them, since I could create toys out of coconut leaves and shells. We made fans, balls, baskets, and mats with the leaves, and castles and imaginary objects with the shells. I could also climb a small coconut tree using a rope tied around my legs. Later when I visited Hawaii, I was amused to find this feat was a tourist attraction.

We depended on the natural world for entertainment. I remember catching dragonflies and tying them to a thread. I would walk them around as if I had a pet. If I met another child, I would play with his dragonfly. Sometimes we had dragonfly fights and they could get serious, like a cockfight, but they were lots of fun.

Using a machete or sickle was no big deal. I had a small sickle about five inches long which I always carried with me to cut branches, slice mangos, or sharpen sticks. I still have that sickle to this day. My son is fascinated with it and we had to order one for him during our recent trip to India.

We often spent almost whole days picking up mangos and cashew nuts from the neighborhood. The mango trees were huge and as children we could not climb them. So we waited for the wind to rise, toss the branches around, and shake the ripe fruit to the ground. We'd gather around the mango tree during the windy season, and the fastest runner usually got the booty. At the end of the day I usually had a couple of mangos in the pockets of my shorts and one or two in my hands. Back home, my mother or Grandmother would scold me when she saw the sap staining my shorts, since I owned only two pairs, one for school and the other for home.

The worst stains came from the bright red and yellow cashew fruits that the nuts were attached to. Yet it was worth the price to collect cashew nuts from the compound and savor the delicious meat. We not only ate cashew nuts by roasting them on a campfire, but we also played with them. If I walked around the neighborhood and met other kids with cashew nuts, all it took to start a game was to dig a putting hole and mark a line four feet away. We tossed the nuts toward the hole and if I, for instance, got the closest to it I had the chance to throw another cashew at all the other nuts lying around the hole. If I hit one I could pocket all of them, and if I missed it the next person got the chance.

I had no shoes or slippers until I was in fourth grade and I was used to going barefoot. It had advantages and disadvantages. The big advantage was that the family did not have to buy shoes or worry about me losing them at school. Over time the soles of my feet became tough enough that shoes seemed unnecessary. And when you waded through streams and jumped into the river many times a day, shoes could get in the way. If you stepped on a thorn, you just pulled it out. If the wound bled, you plucked some leaves, crushed them, and pressed them against the cut. You limped your way home and someone extracted the thorn with the edge of a knife and safety pins.

But one day I stepped on a big thorn and it penetrated deep into my heel. The wound throbbed painfully and neighbors had to carry me home. There, the usual approach didn't work and small fragments remained embedded in my heel. Using the kitchen knife, Grandmother cut the calluses near the entry point and made a circle around it. A dark spot became visible and to remove the thorn completely she worked like a precision sculptor with a safety pin sterilized in flame. The wound started bleeding and she pressed a piece of cloth against it. A sensation of relief passed through me but I noticed that I could feel every heartbeat in my heel.

"This kind of thorn will cause infection," Grandmother told my aunt.

I thought I would go to a hospital a few miles away where they could prevent infection and control the pain. But Grandmother said she would handle it, since she had treated this kind of injury successfully before. She asked the servant girl to make a poultice with rice and salt and apply it to my heel. The salt stung a little but I felt good with this moist lump on my wound.

Then I saw our lady servant coming towards me with a lamp and a wick of cotton roll. She dipped the tip of the roll in oil and lit it from the lamp she brought in from the kitchen. Grandmother took the lighted wick and asked me to lie down.

I noticed that our lady servant was clamping my legs down and my aunt was holding me down also. I was told that if we heated the damp poultice the wound would heal faster and without infection.

Grandmother started tapping the poultice on my wound with the lighted wick. Again it felt good at first, but as the taps continued I began feeling an electrical impulse surging up my legs into my spine. I started howling and the two people keeping me down helped Grandmother ignore my yells as she continued her heat therapy.

The pain reached the top of my head like a lightning bolt. With each tap my cries rose in volume and turned into screams to let me go.

Finally she ceased but the pain lasted for hours. Grandmother's face had a look of satisfaction that the wound would soon heal. I walked on my toes for a few days, the wound in fact did heal, and the calluses returned so I could explore my world again with my feet.

Later in life, I realized that these procedures could take place under local anesthetic using antibiotic ointments — with little agony. I kept this incident in the back of my mind and pledged that any treatment I gave patients would be the least painful possible.

CHAPTER 5

Bhaskaran

We had two servants: Ammini and Bhaskaran Nair. I have known Bhaskaran since I was born. He lived less than a mile away with his wife and children, who were the same age as my older brothers. I remember him in his 30s, a well-built man with strong muscles from the manual labor he performed for our family. He had dark hair and a mustache, and he smoked cigarettes whenever he had a spare minute. He wore a towel around his head like a turban while he worked. He also used it to dust off a chair before sitting down, to make a pillow when he lay down, and to fan himself in the heat.

For many years during my childhood, Bhaskaran was my only male companion. Ever since I can remember, I followed him wherever he went. He took me to the barbershop, the market, the river for swimming, and sometimes to school. I ate lunch with him on the weekends, sitting on a mat on the floor. He gave me personal attention and cared for me. He scolded me when necessary and kept me away from the company of bad kids in the neighborhood. He always had a special fondness for me.

He hurt me only once, when I was seven and asked him to give me a cigarette to smoke. He held out the cigarette to me and I spread my fingers to seize it, copying the way he held a cigarette. I didn't realize he was handing me the lighted end. The cigarette burned the tender flesh between my thumb and forefinger. He told me that even though he smoked, the habit was unhealthy and I should never start. The burn left a scar on my hand and to this day I believe it was a painful but valuable lesson from a sincere, loyal servant. Needless to say, I never smoked.

Bhaskaran was also our caretaker for many years. Grandmother sent him to our relatives' homes with messages as he knew all our friends and kin from far and near. He was a watchman during calving season, sleeping in the verandah waiting for early signs of the cows' water breaking. He killed chickens when special guests visited. He was a handyman in many ways, but he mainly looked after the tapioca plants and rice fields we owned. These needed seeding, timely planting, fertilization, weeding, and watering, and he hired workers to dig up the tapioca roots and cook, dry, and sell them.

Tapioca, or the cassava root, is the staple food of Kerala. Boiled tapioca and fish curry met the nutritional needs of even the poorest people in Kerala. Few people starved, as they did in other parts of India, because fish were abundant and tapioca would grow on even a tiny plot of land.

Bhaskaran also helped with coconuts. During the peak season, other workers climbed the trees using a loop of rope tied around their feet. They collected the coconuts, piled them in heaps on one side of the courtyard, and removed the husks by smashing the coconuts on a metal pole in the ground. Then they cracked the shell, drained off the delicious juice for drinking, and left the open nut in the hot sun.

Once dried, the white, fleshy meat formed "copra," which is rich in oil. Bhaskaran took sacks of copra to the local mill and brought back coconut oil in big jars which we stored carefully in one room of the house and used for cooking all year long. Sometimes we sold the oil to neighbors or small merchants depending on the size of the crop.

We also sold the husks, consisting of fibers called coir, for others to make items ranging from rope to baskets and mattresses. They could also use the husk for scrubbing and cleaning pots and pans.

When the time came for me to go to medical school, Bhaskaran left his wife and children and came to stay with me. I shared a house with four other medical students. He cooked, cleaned, and kept me company for four years.

Bhaskaran has been a blessing to our family and there are not enough words to express the loyalty and sincerity he showed us. To this day we keep in touch and I help him financially. There are certain things in life that money cannot buy and Bhaskaran's devotion is one.

Chapter 6

Thatching the Roof

Every one or two years we started seeing patterns of light on the floor. Sunbeams were breaking through the coconut-leaf roof, which was slowly disintegrating, and during light rains Ammini had to place basins around the house to collect the leaking water. We needed a new roof, and timing was crucial. The monsoon rains were torrential and the new thatching had to be in place before they began.

Thatching was always a memorable event. It was a whole day's job, the combined effort of skilled roofers and neighbors, men and women. (The less-skilled workers thatched the chicken coop and the lean-to for storing firewood and garden tools.) I was allowed to skip school that day to enjoy the activities.

We prepared in advance for this momentous occasion. First we cut fresh green coconut fronds from the trees, split them in two along the midrib, and trimmed the edges. Then, on the day before, we brought these soaked, trimmed coconut leaves into the courtyard. The women wove them diagonally with the shiny side facing up because it was water-repellent. They stacked the woven leaves neatly, ready for placement. Ammini also made sure to store away plenty of drinking water and cover the furniture with sheets.

Next day at dawn there was a festive atmosphere as the lead roofer arrived with his helpers. The neighbors joined them and they tore the dry, old, brittle leaves down from the roof. It was a messy process. Three or four people climbed onto the roof, being careful to step only on the wooden supports so they wouldn't plunge through the thatch. Then they started cutting down the old leaves, letting them drop down to catchers in the courtyard below.

Once the old roof was gone, they began putting the new one in place. They'd send down instructions in different tones, shouting, yelling, and begging. The throwers tossed the mats up so a person could easily catch them. The men on the rooftop carefully tied the woven mats one by one to the wooden structure underneath. They placed extra leaves at the corners and edges to keep water from leaking and wind from lifting the leaves. Meanwhile, the women wove special lengths of mat for reinforcement.

As a boy, all I had to do was walk around the house and watch everyone work, waiting for the feast to begin. For another group of people was preparing this meal outside. They arranged big stones in a circle to create a fire pit, stacked wood in the center, and lit a blaze.

They brought in huge round cooking vessels, full of rice, lentils, beef, and green bananas. I watched fascinated as plumes of steam rose from the boiling rice. A rich, spicy fragrance pervaded the air, from the small, perfectly shaped cubes of beef infused with coriander, cinnamon, cloves, cardamom, and black pepper; the chunks of green banana bubbling in turmeric, cumin, and shredded coconut; and the thin vermicelli noodles simmering in coconut milk, sugar syrup, and cardamom.

By early afternoon the workers had completed the roof, and everyone sang and cheered. To my impressionable young mind, it sounded like an orchestra. Grandmother and Bhaskaran carefully inspected the roof to make sure that all the pieces were in place.

Now everyone awaited the feast. People sat in a row with banana leaves spread before them. Servers placed scoops of rice on the leaves and poured lentil curry on top of them, followed by vegetables and beef. We ate this savory food avidly and washed it down with a hot drink made of boiling cumin seeds in water. Cumin seeds were considered to improve digestion and boiling the infusion purified the water. I felt the whole day was happy as I sat with the workers and ate to my stomach's full capacity. The meal ended with the vermicelli *payasam*, my favorite dessert.

After the feast, many workers headed for the shade. They took out betel nut and tobacco leaves from their pocket, and sat leaning under a tree or against a rock chewing the tobacco and dozing off. Meanwhile, the head roofer walked around the house, trimming a bit here, tightening a knot there, and instructing his assistant to tuck extra leaves in certain places. We paid the workers, and Grandmother presented a new *mundu*, a sarong-like piece of clothing, to the head roofer and towels to his assistants. Poor Ammini spent the rest of the day cleaning up the mess and putting things back in order.

After we moved to Tiruvalla our house had a tiled roof and I never took part in a roof-thatching again. However, these events remain vivid in my mind.

Chapter 7

Lifelines

As a medical professional, I know there are some universal truths. When the body bleeds it goes into shock and when the mind bleeds it goes into depression. Did I suffer depression from all my emotional trials? Not in childhood, because you need only a few words of reassurance from loved ones that you will be important to the family in the future, and that you have someone to love and care for you now.

That love came from my maternal grandfather, P.I. Joseph, the man I was named after. He was a towering individual, in stature and personality. He stood six feet tall, unusual for a Malayalee, and he had a fair complexion. His clothes were always crisp and well-pressed, and I can still see his looming figure in a white *mundu* and white shirt with gold cufflinks and a shawl around his neck.

He had a commanding presence and immediately inspired respect. Nobody messed with him. At the same time, he was the most loving father and grandfather. He was there for a person's marriage, from the proposal to the ceremony. He was there for all births in our family. He was there for all his grandchildren's educational and emotional needs. He guided and molded us, and each of us felt we were his favorite grandchild.

Grandfather visited me once a month and announced his arrival by shouting my name from the edge of our property. Or he would startle the neighbors by his very loud sneeze. When he saw me, he would hug me and keep me close by his side. He tousled my hair, checked my teeth, and occasionally pulled out a loose tooth. He asked about my grades in school, praised me, and encouraged me to keep up the good work. He also made sure that Grandmother was properly caring for me. I heard a few arguments between them about me and my upbringing.

I was unable to live under his guardianship because in those days Kerala tradition dictated that children stay in their paternal home. It would have been considered shameful if I stayed with him while my father's mother was still alive. But looking back, he was always there for me wherever I lived, whether at Grandmother's, in my sister's house, or in boarding school. I was blessed to have a grandfather like him to keep me from sliding into depression because of my emotional deprivation.

The other great support came from the visits of my two brothers during holidays from their boarding school. George and Philip were nine and eight years older than me. On the day of their arrival, I would stand at the top of the property line near the road to catch a glimpse of them. As soon as I spotted them on the road, I ran to them. They embraced me and a sense of security crept into my being. They tossed me in the air and I pestered them to tell me what presents they had for me in their bags.

I always felt a sense of celebration during their visits. The menu changed and Ammini made sure to put meat or fish on the table, as opposed to regular days when we made do with lentils and vegetables. My brothers requested certain foods and their wishes were granted. Bhaskaran was around more to fulfill their demands.

I shadowed my brothers wherever they went on their vacation time and my horizon expanded. We went to the river every day, jumped around, and swam to our hearts' content without restrictions from Grandmother. I noticed that she seemed to grow mellower when they were there. She did not intimidate them because they were older and less vulnerable.

One of my best memories is fishing with them. I don't know if we did it for fun or to really catch fish for the table. To me, the time spent with them was more precious than the motive. Bhaskaran got the bait: earthworms caught from the moist earth by the river. You could detect their presence by the consistency of the soil. Then you just dug, seized them, and put them in a bottle. After that, all you needed was the right thread and a hook. You threaded the wriggling worm onto the fishhook by its tail. The head end remained free to squirm about in the water and attract the fish. The floater was a piece of stem from a banana tree.

I was only allowed to sit next to them and watch. I received strict instructions not to enter the water or disturb the fish. My job was to keep watch of the fish they caught and stored in a basket next to me. They often whistled to attract the fish, although I don't know if this tactic had any effect. When we returned home, everyone's face was glowing with satisfaction. My heart filled with happiness because I felt part of a momentous event in which I was lovingly included.

After two or three weeks, depending on whether it was the Christmas holiday or midterm break, my brothers returned to boarding school and my life reverted to the old routine. I always wonder if my childhood would have been happier if they had been around. But destiny dictated otherwise. Life went on and I waited for the coin to flip and give me better days.

Another happy memory was our summer holidays with my maternal grandparents in the village of Punnaveli. "Punna" is the Malayalam term for a type of tree and "vely" means "fence." Punnavely was famous for its local fences made of logs and branches from the punna trees. It was a typical central Kerala village with rubber tree plantations and paddy fields. The Manimala River flowed through it.

The town was only 15 miles from Mallapally but it took an hour by bus. We then had to walk almost two miles from the bus stop to reach Grandfather's house.

Once at the compound, I rushed up the steep steps to the house in one breath. I have already described Grandfather. He greeted me at the veranda, stroked my forehead, and wiped the sweat away with the towel on his shoulder, and then he announced my arrival to my grandmother in the kitchen. She took me to the kitchen and made sure I had something to drink and ate a snack before I ran outside to see what my cousins were doing.

My little cotton bag had only one or two changes of clothes. They were usually wrinkled and dirty, and my grandmother gave them to the servant girl to make sure they were washed and dried by the end of the day.

The happy times spent in that house will never fade from my memory. There were usually 12 or 15 grandchildren during the summer holidays. Paulose and Awaran, two street boys adopted by my grandfather, supervised us and attended to all our needs during the day. We explored the compound, which had mango trees, jackfruits, cashew nuts, coconut palms, coffee trees, and guavas. Older cousins plucked ripe guavas, then cut and distributed the pieces to the little kids who were watching and waiting. We also waited for the wind to blow mangos from the tree and ran fast to catch them when it did. Back at home, my grandmother sliced and distributed them equally to all the grandkids. Sometimes if we got a really ripe one, we bit the stalk off with our teeth and sucked the pulp.

We enjoyed many other activities. We were allowed to swim in the canal in front of that house, but my grandfather ordered the older cousins to watch the little ones very closely, as he had lost a grandson in that canal a few years before. We often walked along the narrow edge of the paddy field, placing one foot right in front of the other and balancing carefully so as not to fall into the paddy itself. We visited the neighbors, listened to their stories, and answered their curious questions about our parents. On some days I sat on the wide stalk of a coconut leaf and one of the cousins pulled it like a toboggan up and down the hill, until the stem wore down and you started feeling the sand on your rear.

Grace was the oldest granddaughter. Everyone called her Kunjumol, which meant "little daughter." I called her Njolma. She was about eight years older than me and was like my big sister. She was also a role model in my life. She went to medical school and became an ob-gyn. Njolma recognized my academic potential and encouraged me to study hard, go to medical school, and become a doctor. She did not get much time to play, as she had to help my grandmother prepare lunch and dinner for the whole gang. She made sure that all our clothes were washed and helped the little kids with their baths in the evening. I remember her helping me bathe by the side of the family well. She drew water from the well, tucking her skirt into her waist, scrubbed me with soap, and poured water over me.

Even though there were many servants, Njolma helped my grandmother serve dinner to all the cousins and my grandmother made sure everyone had enough. Food was abundant in my grandfather's house. He was a landowner and a rich man in the community, and we had plenty of meat and fish at every meal no matter how many grandkids were sitting around the table.

After dinner, Njolma gathered all of us for family prayer. She and the older cousins read from the Bible. My grandfather corrected them if they stumbled on a word, and he prayed for each of us and mentioned our parents far away in the Persian Gulf. My grandmother's sweet voice led us in singing hymns.

At bedtime, Njolma made sure we had sheets and pillows. She supervised the servant girl in the kitchen as she cleaned all the vessels, and made sure the pots and pans were filled with drinking water. My grandmother soaked rice to make pancakes for breakfast. My grandfather retired with a fan in his hand and occasionally shouted to my grandmother asking her to bring water or refill the kerosene in the flickering lamp. The cousins gathered in groups according to their ages and retired for the night in different parts of the house.

Njolma's younger brother Josekuttychayan (Dr. Joseph John, now a urologist in Oman) was a great storyteller. He used to come to our bedside and begin with, "Once upon a time there was a king." He'd describe beautiful castles and princes on horseback. His younger sister Alice would interrupt with questions, which occasionally irritated him. If he stopped to explain the story to her, I reminded him where he had left off. The story continued and usually had a happy ending.

As he spoke, we often dozed off before he left our bedside. Njolma walked around and shone her lamp to see if we were sleeping. If my eyes were open, she would kneel by my bed, rub my head, pat my back, and reassure me that everything was okay and it was time for me to sleep.

I never had to stay vigilant in that house, listening for noises and worrying about ghosts, as the stories I heard were happy ones. The events of the day and the love and care I received all helped ease me to sleep with no anxiety. If I woke up in the middle of the night, I often heard my grandmother whispering to my grandfather or singing spiritual songs in a very low voice, only to be interrupted by questions from my grandfather about the next day's plans and the menu for the kids. The times I spent in that house were the happiest days of my childhood and enough to recharge me for the many lonely months in my other grandmother's house in Mallapally.

CHAPTER 8

New Student at M.G.M. High

Then my life changed dramatically. My father built another home for us in 1958. It was a two-story building in a good location in Tiruvalla, a larger town with a railway station, Christian school, reputable college, medical mission hospital, and downtown all within walking distance.

From fifth to eighth grade I attended the local day school in Tiruvalla, still staying with Grandmother and my widowed aunt in the new house. The school routine was unremarkable and my grades were average. During eighth grade, Father sent Mother home for a year to supervise my studies.

Suddenly, a letter arrived with the news that Father had fainted in the office. He had diabetes. His doctor urged that Mother be with him to take care of his health, as there were no hotels or cafeterias at his workplace to provide the proper diet.

As usual, Mother had to shuffle things around. My brother said he would stay in a lodge and he found a boarding school for me. The family decided that since I was entering high school I should not have any more distractions. My younger sister Molly went to a girls' boarding school.

In retrospect, my boarding school days shaped me for life.

The first day my brother dropped me off at the entrance, I looked up and read "M.G.M. High School" on the signboard. The school had a spacious, quiet campus with a football field, away from the hustle and bustle of the town center.

The boarding master, Mr. T.M. Thomas, welcomed me and introduced me to the other students. The semester had already started, but the school had admitted me as a special case due to my family emergency. There were three rooms with shelves to keep suitcases and the boarding master pointed out a space on a shelf for my own.

He took me to the classroom and I was the object of curious stares from students. I saw the questions in their eyes: Where did this character come from to intrude on and disrupt our class? The teacher pointed to a bench and I quietly sat down and listened to what he was teaching. It was algebra.

When the bell rang at the end of school, the day scholars headed home and the boarding students went back to the suitcase room to store their books and change clothes. Behind the suitcase room was the mess hall and the tables had coffee for students who wanted it. But most of them ran out to the sports field to play soccer or badminton.

I had always liked soccer so I went to see the game. As the new kid, I watched from the sidelines and occasionally kicked the ball back to the field. After few days, seeing my kicking form and energy, they invited me into the game and soon they picked me for the team to play in the inter-scholastic league.

At the end of the evening, students lined up to wash. Only the senior students got the showers and the rest of the crowd gathered around the water tank. We passed the bucket around, and there was pushing, shoving, and yelling until the boarding master showed up.

Then we changed into our nightclothes and headed to study hall. After the evening prayer there was pin-drop silence in the hall from 6 to 8 o'clock except for a few whispers and the occasional student moving around to sharpen a pencil or borrow an eraser.

At 8 pm the dinner bell rang. One of the senior students blessed the food and the mess hall staff served dinner. The boarding master always appeared at one point with the announcement for the day and any special events for the week, perhaps a field trip or a visit to a nearby church for a religious festival. On some days he sounded like a mother, telling us how to shampoo our hair, wash between our toes, eat slowly, and chew the food. He loved the students and the students returned his affection and respected him. He was also a football coach and to get his attention you just had to ask a question about sports or his experience with a school team. You could get away with anything on those occasions as he encouraged students to take part in sports while we studied hard to keep up our grades.

At 8:30, we were back in the study hall till 9.30 pm when the last bell rang for bedtime. We had mattresses tucked under benches in the study hall, which now became the dormitory (and which would serve as the classroom next day). Students rolled their beds out on the floor and slowly the noise level fell as the lights dimmed. Occasionally, we spotted the boarding master strolling around with his flashlight to make sure everyone was in bed.

When the rising bell sounded at 6 am, we all woke up, rolled up our beds, stuck them under the benches, and headed to the suitcase room for bathroom routines and morning shower. Black coffee was available in the mess hall and by 7 am we were back in the study hall for an hour of studying. We ate breakfast between 8 and 9, and school started at 9 am. Saturdays were almost like regular school days as we were expected to spend the time studying and doing our homework. Sundays were for church activities and visitors. There were no weekends for goofing off.

I liked the routine from the very first day and enjoyed the time dedicated to regular studies with no distractions, unlike home where there was no specified time for studying. Before boarding school, I did only the minimum homework required when prompted by Mother. I never studied actively. But being with focused students who worked hard day and night changed my study habits. The boarding school routine became deeply embedded in me for the rest of my student days and it helped me tackle the difficult medical school curriculum.

Though I hadn't had much interaction with my father in those days, I had heard his constant advice to my brothers to always do their best. "If you are going to be a barber, be the best in town," he used to say. "If you are going to be a drummer, be the best in your field. If you are going to be a handyman, make sure you have all the skills and tools to excel in your work." That advice permeated our family. Boarding school sharpened it for me and I have lived by it all my life.

Among the students there, M.C. Thomas was the role model. At least once a week, the boarding master pointed out something outstanding he had done that the rest of us should emulate. He had been first in his class since grade five. I noticed his study habits. He took meticulous notes in class and rewrote them during study hall. On Saturdays he reviewed the chapters covered that week and previewed those for the next week. I greatly envied the attention he received. He never took part in sports but used all his spare time to study. I liked everything he did, but I could not give up my playtime.

One day I rashly blurted out in front of some students that I could beat M.C. Thomas in the next semester exam. The news spread throughout the school and I started feeling unusual pressure. At the end of the semester the exam results came out. The teachers always called out the names of the students in the order of their rank in class. Thomas had the highest mark and Boban Joseph had the second highest. I heard my name called next and the teacher remarked that there was now another student who could shine in the state final exams and bring credit to the school.

Though I hadn't beaten him, I was filled with confidence that day. This achievement fostered my competitive spirit. I continued to excel in academics, and we maintained the same rank order even for the state level final exam. I received a first class on this test, a prestigious honor for any student and his family. My own family members, especially my father, rejoiced since we knew that I could now apply to a college of my choice.

Boarding school equipped me well for the rest of my student life. I learned the value of discipline and postponed gratification to achieve higher goals. I learned from others who succeeded. The saying that there is a time for everything was true in boarding school. There was a time for study and a time for play, a time to relax and a time to pray and plan, a time to exercise and a time for friendship. The experience especially prepared me for medical school, as success there depended on your ability to focus on studies and keep up with the curriculum.

CHAPTER 9

The Raging Elephant and the Tiger Claw

During the first semester break, I had a brush with death. It would not be my only one, or my worst, but I'll never forget it. Our own house was locked up and I could visit any of my relatives for the holidays. My older sister Lilly is like my mother and she is very fond of me. I had heard stories about her wanting to return to our house the week after she got married to look after me, as I was a baby at that time. So I decided to spend my vacation at her place.

It was harvest festival time in Kerala and Lillykochamma[1] was the one to be around during festivals. She was very outgoing and caring, and her charm and affection were legendary among our relatives. She had married a man from a very reputable family, and he and his two brothers owned many rubber, tea, and coffee plantations. Their home lay near forests in Kerala and it was almost like a vacation resort.

After an hour by bus, I had to walk a few miles to reach their estate. The road went uphill and as I neared her home, the neighbors recognized me as Lillykochamma's brother and stopped for small talk. Then one of my nephews spotted me from the top of the hill and shouted to my sister that Uncle had arrived. Lillykochamma came running to me, put her hands

---

1 "Kochamma" is a term of respect used to address older female relatives. It literally means "little mother," and Lillykochamma embodied this concept completely.

on my shoulders, and kissed both my cheeks. She took me to the kitchen and gave me a diluted form of yogurt, spiced with salt and ginger: the best pick-me-up for replenishing electrolytes after a hot, tiring walk. She usually had a special treat to snack on, and there were always bunches of bananas and gigantic jackfruit in the storage area. The kids crowded around to hear about boarding school news.

Lillykochamma's house stood in the middle of one of the lushest rubber estates I can remember. She and her husband owned the best one in that area. The straight trunks and thick green leaves of the trees formed a dense canopy, and even at noon no direct sunlight reached the ground. The house was always cool during day and at night we heard the leaves rustling around the estate.

We didn't waste much time but immediately started exploring the estate, meeting the workers, and satisfying my curiosity about recent developments such as new plants, pest control, and sap collection. The helicopter flying over the estate to fertilize the trees always attracted kids to gaze at it.

Kuttappan was the chief worker there and he had been with them for many years. Early in the morning the workers went around the estate reopening cuts in the trunks to free the flow of white latex. The latex drained into a coconut shell placed between two metal plates inserted in the trunk under the cut. By noon the workers came back to collect the latex in small buckets and take it to the factory on the premises. There they dried the latex in flat metal pans to form sheets of rubber. Machines then pressed them thin to send to vendors.

At my request Kuttappan asked one of the workers to make a rubber ball out of the dried up strands of latex. I kept this toy in my pocket wherever I went during the holidays, and we played soccer, cricket, and many other games with it. Once one of us threw the ball down in anger or frustration. It bounced up almost to the greenery and we heard my brother-in-law yell that it would damage the precious leaves. He smiled to reassure me that I was not the culprit, but that his children who had grown up among rubber trees should have known better.

So we moved on to a quieter area, down at the end of the complex among the rubber and tea factories. It was very smelly in the area where workers collected the latex and dried it into sheets. But at the tea factory, the aroma of roasting tea leaves welcomed us. This was my favorite spot. Even though my nieces and nephews had seen it a thousand times, they went with me to see it again through my eyes.

The workers came by one by one to greet me. Here, the tea leaves arrived from surrounding plantations and were processed into the product we see in retail shops. I saw drying rooms, roasting rooms, shredding rooms, and packing rooms. I don't remember the details of the processing, even though my brother-in-law explained them to me many times. Instead, I remember the periodic thud from the steam room and the constant sound of the heavy fan belts that rolled inside that factory. My brother-in-law understood those noises as a mother does her baby's cry, and from them he could identify the stage of production and the amount of tea that had been processed.

Hunger was the only force that would bring us back home. Otherwise, there were plenty of areas to explore and activities to keep us engaged. Food was plentiful at my sister's house because she provided lunch for the workers. She always had two servants in the kitchen and there were two or three more at her beck and call for special days.

She surpassed herself during Onam. Onam is the harvest festival and, like Thanksgiving in the United States, one of the most celebrated holidays in Kerala. Preparation for the Onam feast started two or three days beforehand. They extended the kitchen out into the courtyard with temporary cooking areas made with stones that could hold big vessels. My favorite item was dessert. I would ask her, "Are you making *payasam*?" She would answer, "I am going to make *payasam* and *pradaman*." They were both kinds of pudding using rice and noodles.

A big swing made of thick, commercial rope hung between two rubber trees near the entrance to the estate. The servants of Thankachayan, my brother-in-law, made sure it was secure and safe for us, and he himself then checked it out by swinging on it. Along with his brother's children, we were the first to break in that swing. Later, the neighborhood kids joined in. As one pushed, the others yelled, "Higher, higher!" The onlookers clapped and sang, and the whole place became festive and lively.

In front of the house the men played the ancient game of *kabadi*. There were two teams. Each occupied the opposite side of the yard and took turns sending a "raider" into the other court to win points by tagging or wrestling members of the opposing team. The raider then tried to return to his own team, chanting, "Kabadi, kabadi, kabadi" without taking a breath. Thankachayan's brother Charlie looked like a wrestler with his handlebar mustache, and everyone wanted him on their team. But the kids were smart and could make him laugh while he was chanting. He would lose his breath and have to return to his side without scoring a point. My nieces Valsamma and Leelamma made sure we had drinks during the games and were very attentive to all other needs like towels or band-aids if someone scratched an elbow.

The game stopped when the Kaduvakali or Tiger Dance troupe arrived. Four men made up the group: two with tiger face-masks and bodies painted yellow, a hunter with a wooden rifle, and a drummer. During Onam, they went from house to house entertaining people and collecting money for their performances. The crowd accompanying them and our own group gathered in the courtyard. The drummer started his rhythmic beat and the two tiger-men prowled the area. Then they dropped to all fours and mimicked a tiger's gait to the rhythm of the drummer. They stalked the hunter and the hunter tried to evade them. The game continued for five or ten minutes until the tigers did cartwheels across the yard and the hunter shouted, "Dakko!" imitating the sound of a gunshot. The tigers froze and played dead, and the crowd clapped and cheered. The troupe collected its money and moved on to the next house. This game might seem politically incorrect today, since tigers are an endangered species, but at the time it was entertaining and exciting, our substitute for comic-book heroes like Spiderman and Superman.

Onam lunch is very special in Kerala homes. As Lillykochamma is renowned for her hospitality, this feast is worth describing. We sat on the floor of the verandah. Banana leaves were placed before each of us, and a scoop of rice was piled onto the leaf. Its aroma wafted up and we keenly anticipated the rest of the fare. Then the servants moved up and down the rows serving the food. First came the vegetarian dishes: *thoran* (beans and shredded coconut), *kalan* (sweet plantain chunks in a thick yogurt spiced with turmeric and cumin), *upperi* (fried banana chips), *papadam* (lentil fritters), *paripukari* (lentil stew with mustard seeds), and *sammanthi* (coconut chutney). Since we were Christians, there were also non-vegetarian items like mutton stew and chicken curry. Throughout, Lillykochamma watched to see if anyone needed seconds.

Then we all waited eagerly for the desserts. As she had promised me, we had *payasam*, or vermicelli cooked in sugar and coconut milk, garnished with raisins and cashew nuts fried in clarified butter. And *pradaman*, a dish served in Hindu temples on very special occasions. You boil rice flakes in brown sugar and coconut milk, and flavor it with cardamom. The *payasam* and *pradaman* put us in a food coma and guests found places to rest after the games and heavy meal.

One day my nephew Raju said, "Let's go see the elephant in my uncle's house next door." Raju was only three years younger than me and we were constant companions in our mischievous school days. As rubber trees only have about 20 years of good yield, Lillykochamma and her husband had contracted out large areas of the estate to timber merchants who uprooted the trees and took away the lumber. Since it was difficult for trucks to navigate between the trees, they used elephants to haul the logs away. They tied a rope around each log and the animal pulled it to the waiting truck. Estate owners allowed elephants to spend the night, as it was believed that their dung improved the harvest in the following year.

We ran to see the elephant. As we entered the courtyard, we smelled the stench of its dung, which permeated the air. The beast was tied to the trunk of a coconut tree with iron chains. We joined the crowd and sat around the elephant in a circle. The mahout, the elephant handler, told the kids not to excite the animal but only to look at it. However, a number of neighborhood kids were teasing it by throwing branches and twigs at it, and occasionally a boy tossed a pebble.

It was fascinating to watch the elephant eating banana leaves and coconut fronds, occasionally throwing the leaves onto its back. It constantly fanned its ears back and forth to keep the flies away. When it turned to one side, the kids facing it jumped up and when the elephant turned to the other side, the kids there jumped up as well. When it urinated, the kids screamed. The elephant appeared a little agitated but the mahout didn't seem concerned and went inside the house to eat lunch.

One boy had a whistle and he blew it loudly. Suddenly the elephant turned toward him and we noticed that the chain that anchored it had become loose. The crowd of children ran in all four directions. Raju and I dashed into his uncle's house leaping onto the three big steps that led to the verandah. Breathing a sigh of relief that I was safe, I turned around.

To my terror, I saw the elephant behind me with its trunk raised, mouth wide open, and front foot on the bottom step of the verandah. In that same instant, I saw the mahout running out of the house. He caught hold of its tusk, led it back to the tree, and secured the chains. To this day I can hear my heart pounding.

When we returned home, Lillykochamma scolded us for joining the rowdy group that provoked the elephant. I had nightmares for many months after that. Even today, when I think about the event, my heart skips a beat as I wonder what would have happened to me if I had stumbled over a stone or missed a step during that panicked run.

The next day a rat catcher (*vetoon*) came to the house. *Vetoons* were a special tribe of people who specialized in this trade and went from house to house practicing it. According to rumor, they ate the rats at the end of the day. The rat catcher was practically naked. He wore only a small towel around his loins and a hat made of palm leaves. After getting permission from Lillykochamma, he walked the grounds blowing smoke into any holes he could find. At the end of the morning he came back with four rats and was paid according to the number of rats he had caught.

We received another memorable visit from the *laaden*, the local medicine man. His knowledge of the location of medicinal plants had been handed down from generation to generation, and he often went into the forest to collect exotic plants to make ointments. A turban covered his head and he wore many necklaces made of dried berries deemed to have healing powers.

The *laaden* announced his arrival by singing chants proclaiming his possession of herbal medicines and ointments for many illnesses. After setting his sack on the verandah he took out a dry broomstick, broke it into pieces, and showed how brittle it was. Then he rubbed one of his oils onto a splinter and bent it to show that it now did not break. He explained that he had medicine to cure broken bones, aching muscles, and chronic headaches. Lillykochamma purchased peacock oil, which supposedly helped bruises. He urged people to buy his bear oil but nobody wanted it.

Raju asked the *laaden* whether he had any remedy for my fear of darkness. His eyes twinkled. He reached deep down in his bag and pulled out a claw. He said it was a tiger claw and if I wore it on a chain, I would not be afraid anymore. Everyone laughed, but I took it seriously. Even if it turned out to be just a superstition, I wanted it and bought it. Fear of darkness and a sense of abandonment had opened deep wounds in my psyche and I thought, "What can I lose?"

Almost like a child clinging to a blanket, I have that tiger claw to this day. I no longer need it for the reason I bought it and I don't even know if it is real. A few years ago, I had it dipped in gold and made it into a pendant that I wear occasionally as a conversation piece.

Overall, my time at Lillykochamma's house was very nurturing and I did not miss my parents as she took care of all my needs like a mother.

CHAPTER 10

The Old Man Under the Mango Tree

Since I was born into a Christian family and grew up in it, my spiritual journey was Christian. My mother taught me from the Bible that people with spirituality had good, observable traits, like love, joy, peace, kindness, faithfulness, gentleness, and self-control. I memorized this list and meditated on it throughout my life.

All living things go through the cycle of creation, birth, growth, change, decay, and destruction. My logical mind told me that the spiritual realm might also follow this sequence. But the mystery of the soul remains and the hope we have varies from person to person.

In my childhood I made some observations about spirituality. In the river where I bathed, I saw people looking at the sun, holding their hands together, and chanting. I heard that this was sun worship. I saw people vocalizing mantras in the temple. I heard that they were followers of the god in that temple. I listened to the beautiful music and liturgical recital of prayers and burning of the incense in the local church in my village. I heard that these were the faithful offering their prayer to God, led by their priest. I often saw the village butcher, Mamooka, a well-built man with a long beard and hat, kneeling in front of his shop during the day. Bhaskaran, a Hindu, used to come from the temple with a sandalwood mark on his forehead. He told me it was paste made at the feet of an idol in the temple and it bestowed peace and prosperity on him. He brought *prasa-dam*, food blessed at the temple, and gave it to me for good luck. From the storybooks I knew that primitive tribes believed in a "flow of energy," an unutterable power infused in the material world. It pervaded the harvest, hunting, food, wind, storm, and rain, and could bring protection from nature's "anger." I have since attended charismatic churches where people clap and raise their hands, saying, "Praise the Lord!" and "Halleluiah!" I understood from childhood that these were all expressions of the spiritual-ity of different people. I was convinced that one's religion and belief system dictated them.

When I started going to Sunday school and listened to the stories in the Bible, I felt that spirituality had a magic and mystery. When Moses stretched his staff out on the Red Sea and it parted, I sensed that spiritual-ity had power over nature. When Jonah was swallowed by a whale and spit forth after three days, I knew that spirituality had a purpose. When I heard about Daniel in the lion's den, I knew that spirituality gives protection by the Almighty. When I heard about Joshua and the walls of Jericho tum-bling, I saw that spirituality had power to conquer. When I heard of David killing the mighty Goliath, I felt that spirituality enables the impossible. When I heard the story of Jesus feeding the five thousand with five loaves of bread, the magic of spirituality was captivating and I wanted to know more about this Jesus. During Christmas season the songs and prayers played out a theme that God became flesh and dwelt among us.

One of the Hindu maharishis in India teaches that spirituality is self-realization and self-perfection. To achieve these goals we need a religion. However, an atheist friend of mine said, "Religion is for powerless people like you, who want to depend on something all the time," adding, "It just has a tranquillizing effect for you and it is a waste of time."

I did not have much debating skill in those days, so I replied that I was happy to be among the majority of powerless people and lead my life acknowledging that there is a higher power than me. I asked him how he chose between good and evil if he didn't have a religion. He replied that all you need is common sense. So where did I get this common sense? Was it from home, the classroom, or a religious congregation?

In our circle of family and church we had landmark days signaling the beginnings of our spiritual journey: the day we were "born again" and the day we were baptized. The date of my baptism was June 4, 1967, and I was "born again" in 1961, when I was in eighth grade. I don't recall the exact date, but I remember the experience very well.

One Sunday my mother rushed me to get ready to go to church. We never missed Sunday worship if we were well, but I felt vaguely ill and asked if I could stay home. She put a hand on my forehead and told me to stick out my tongue. I had no fever, she declared, but I could stay home if I didn't feel up to par. When she returned from church she put her hand on my neck and said I did have a fever. She wanted me to eat, but I wasn't hungry. She thought these were bad signs and took me to the local hospital.

Tiruvalla Medical Mission Hospital was just a 15-minute walk from my home. Built in 1931 by missionaries, it was an icon of healing in our area and it had a spiritual foundation. Its motto was to share the compassion of Christ with the sick and offer affordable healthcare services. Many patients testified that they got hope as well as healing from the dedicated physicians and nurses there.

Ever since moving to Tiruvalla we had often visited this hospital to see relatives or friends admitted as patients. I observed its every activity in detail. The big car porch led you to the lobby, where patients congregated waiting for clinics and pharmacy and laboratory tests. The corridors thronged with nurses pacing back and forth from the central sterilizing room carrying syringes and medicines in a kidney-shaped tray and heading to patients' rooms. The orderlies moved patients through the same corridor, which led to the special private rooms.

Since it was Sunday the lobby was not that busy and we saw the doctor soon. He told my mother that I had a fever of 102 and had to be admitted to the hospital for observation. "Anijan's ward," I heard my mother tell the doctor. That is where I wound up.

The general ward had 50 beds arranged in a row in a big hall, but there were more comfortable, private rooms that the family could rent at a daily rate. The medical bills escalated depending on the room you chose. So the amount of money you could spend dictated your place in a hospital back then.

Anijan's ward was an affordable area for an average household. The rooms had no doors and curtains gave patients all the privacy they had. The bed and a side-table were the sole furnishings in that room. A few tears rolled down my mother's cheek when they wheeled me in, and I saw her wipe them off with the end of her sari. She sent the servant girl back home to bring a small mattress, pillow, bed sheet, and towel for my stay.

A nurse came into my room with a clipboard and my chart. In those days nurses were like Florence Nightingale to me. Dressed in a white uniform and white cap, they wore a watch with a second hand to check the pulse and had a special aura. She had a kidney tray in her hand and I knew it was time for an injection. The nurse said the doctor had ordered procaine penicillin for me and I had to bare my bottom. I have not gotten over fear of the needle and injection even today, but my mother held my hand and I took the shot without much fuss.

Next day my fever came down and I felt better. My mother went home to get lunch by mid-morning. I was in the room with a fellow patient when I saw Brother Abraham walk in. He was in his fifties and we called him Avarachen Upadesy. I had seen him in the hospital lobby preaching to the crowd in loud, charismatic tones. At mid-morning every day, he usually stopped all activities in the lobby for five minutes and with his brassy voice he prayed for the people assembled there and gave them a gospel message. He was the equivalent of the hospital chaplain and his call was evangelism for the sick and needy. The rest of the time he went around visiting patients and distributing brochures for spiritual promotion. He was also a good family friend so his visit did not surprise me.

He tapped on my shoulder and sat next to my bed on a stool. He inquired about Mother and asked how I was feeling. After the initial talk, he asked whether I attended Sunday school and introduced the mystery question: "Are you born again?"

I had heard the term several times but never thought anyone would confront me with that question. My negative answer prompted him to open the Bible to the Gospel of John chapter three and read me the story of a famous Jewish leader called Nicodemas who, when Jesus asked him the question, responded, "How can a man be born again? Does he have to go back into his mother's womb?"

Avarachen Upadesy explained to me that being born again was a transformation in the heart rather than a physical rebirth. It was the conviction that God had a plan for us and had provided Jesus as our savior. Even though the information was already in my mind, that day I prayed with him and promised that I would increase my knowledge and understanding of this mystery.

That was the beginning of my spiritual journey — in a hospital bed with a man who barely had high school education walking around with a beaten up Bible in his hand and inspiring people to look into the mystery of being born again.

But it was an old man under a mango tree who directed me onto the path of spiritual growth.

All growth needs nourishment and spiritual growth is no exception. I knew that the main source for it was hearing the word of God written in the Bible. Avarachen Upadesi had told me to read the Bible daily, but it had no appeal to me. Bible reading was routine at our home before the evening prayer and there was nothing unusual or moving about it. I accepted it since my parents revered the Bible and I respected their routine. But whenever I tried to read a portion, I found the sentences long, the language wooden, and stories familiar from repeated exposure.

As people use fortune cookies to predict their future, I have used the Bible by closing my eyes, opening the book, and randomly touching a verse. If my finger landed on a good verse, I assumed I would have a good day. Back then, it did not make sense that reading the Bible might improve my spiritual growth. My passions were outdoor activities like competing in soccer, playing with a tennis ball, swimming in the canal, and simply walking along the railway line till I found something interesting to do.

About ten minutes from my home, there was a big house that belonged to Mr. P.V. George. If I left the gate of my house with a tennis ball in my pocket, Mother assumed that I would be going there. Before his death, Mr. George had been the patriarch of the Pynumootil family, and an evangelist and an orator who played a major role in the Christian reformation movements in Kerala. At that time I would never have guessed that I would one day marry Mr. P.V. George's grandniece! His widow and my mother were friends and I had permission to go to their place and play with other kids any time.

The house was large and had an extensive grassy front yard. At its edge stood a huge mango tree, one of the biggest trees I remember from those days. It had three branches sticking out at a lower level and one that slanted up almost 45 degrees from the ground. With its inviting form and slope, the branch invited you to relax on it. The grassy ground and the shade from the massive tree attracted a few kids who turned it into a play area, and the lady of the house tolerated us nuisances, as she knew all the children.

Often I saw an old man sitting on a folded blanket under that mango tree reading the Bible. He had white hair and always wore a corduroy jacket over the white traditional attire of the local people. One day he clapped and beckoned the children playing in the yard. He asked us to sit down and he read from the Book of Psalms. His voice was very soft but I felt affection in it. Then he asked us if anyone could recite a segment from the Bible. None of us volunteered to show our ignorance in front of this scholarly-looking wise man. So he made a deal: If anyone could memorize a portion and recite it next day, he would give us 50 paisa.

Wow, ice cream money! That was all I thought at the time. The bicycle ice cream vendor's route ran through this compound and his blowing horn never mattered to me as I had no money. So I took up the offer and started memorizing small sections from the Book of Psalms.

On the days I made mistakes I got only 25 paisa. One day the old man asked us to start memorizing eight verses from Psalms 119. One in particular left a strong mark in my mind. In essence, it said: How can a young lad lead a clean life? The answer was by carefully reading the Word and obeying it. Even in my old age that message still stays with me. I don't remember much of the other portions I memorized, but I did relish many ice creams those days. Ice cream was the carrot this wise man used to teach me a lifelong habit. So an old man under the mango tree planted the practice of reading psalms and memorizing them. His name was Benjamin Master and he was the father of Mrs. P.V. George.

One summer vacation when I was a teenager I attended a Bible camp in Irinjalakuda, 30 miles from Cochin. The campus was big and serene for such a retreat, and 25 students attended the ten-day session of intense Bible study.

The camp director was evangelist C.V. Samuel from Dindigal, a famous orator and a renowned Bible teacher. He was charming and his classes interested me. He taught us good techniques for studying the book and the classes encouraged and edified me.

One evening he summoned me and a friend to his room. Looking stern, he asked us to sit down. "You broke the Eighth Commandment," he said in a grim voice.

My mind went blank. Which one was the Eighth? Was it adultery or stealing? As a Bible student you were supposed to rattle off these Commandments fluently. My friend looked at me, lifting his shoulders. There were no girls in the dorm and I didn't recall jumping any fences.

Then the mess manager appeared and told us that we had taken a coconut and some brown sugar from the kitchen. We replied that it was a basically innocent act and we simply wanted the thrill of eating a full coconut with brown sugar sitting in a remote part of that campus.

The director said, "The Bible teaches, 'Thou shall not steal,'" and added, "You should be punished."

He spoke in almost a King James version of English and we waited to hear the verdict. Even though we live in the New Testament age, I was a bit worried that he might resort to the Old Testament: eye for an eye and tooth for a tooth.

He paused for a long while and then reached out to his shelf and pulled out two legal pads. He said, "Copy Psalm 119 seven times."

Psalm 119, for the student or serious reader, is the Mt. Everest of the Bible. It has 22 sections, each starting with a successive letter of the Hebrew alphabet. Every section has eight verses, for a total of 172 taking up almost eight pages. Who wants to even read it in one sitting?

We filled up two legal pads and returned to our dorm. We were exhausted, humbled, and greatly embarrassed by this experience. After finishing, we not only knew the Commandments in order, but had gone through this chapter far more than the rest of the class. I must say that it all had a dual impact on me. First, I saw that there is no such thing as small stealing and big stealing; there is just stealing. Second, I realized that I had climbed Mt. Everest several times!

All spiritual journeys have surges that help propel you toward your maturity. They may be remarkable occurrences, distinctive individuals, or trials. In our community, revival meetings were common and prominent evangelists took part in them. Our family was getting ready to go to one of them when an evangelist in a white shirt with a pleated scarf on his shoulder stopped by to meet my grandfather. I had heard of him and I was pleased to see him talking to my grandfather on the veranda. He had an aura and a commanding voice. Mother asked our servant girl to boil milk and she mixed Ovaltine in it and brought cookies and cake for the evangelist. My quota for milk in those days was once a week or less, as milk was not common. When I saw him getting so much attention from my folks, I wanted to go up and shake his hand. I was a young lad and no one bothered to introduce me to him.

We went to the meeting and after the songs the preacher rose to speak. I don't remember many of the details, but his choice of words and the pitch of his voice reverberates in my memory. He periodically pointed upward and said one day there would be a thunder in the sky and everyone would hear a great trumpet blast. God would descend and we would be taken to heaven. He also mentioned dead people rising from the grave, but I was more interested in our flight when the Lord appeared above. I remember him repeating "thunder in the sky," and concluding the sermon by giving everybody spiritual hope about eternal life. Spiritual hope is our driving force in life and I had something to visualize early on.

Years later I shook the hands of this famous preacher, K.G. Thomas, and he gave me the hand of his granddaughter Bina, recited the marriage vow, and bestowed on me a partner to share my spiritual hope. In the circle of life a few years later, as the physician in the family, I was at his bedside holding his hands while he took his last breath and returned to the creator and the Lord he loved.

Chapter 11

Summer in Oman

In Muscat my father was working as an insurance surveyor for Gray Mackenzie Company, an agent for the famous Lloyd's of London, and after I graduated from high school in 1964 he arranged for my younger sister Molly and me to visit him. My uncle's daughter Alice, who was Molly's age, came along since her mother also worked in Muscat.

We boarded a train in Kerala and after a two-day journey reached Bombay, where my father's brother Mathai welcomed us at Victoria Terminal. We stayed with him for a few days while he obtained the necessary visas from the Oman embassy.

We went down to board the S.S. *Dumra*. Uncle worked in the port and he knew all the formalities for minimizing the hassle. He escorted us to our cabin and said our trip to Muscat would take four days and three nights. We had a port of call in Karachi, Pakistan, and he told us to stay on the ship when it docked there. In fact, he sternly warned us not to disembark for any reason until we saw our father in Muscat.

We set sail from Bombay on a bright sunny day. The *Dumra* had about 50 cabins and hundreds of deck passengers who paid a nominal fare for the voyage. They brought their own sleeping bags and slept outside. We had a cabin that accommodated three people, with two bunk beds on one side and a regular bed on the other.

As I had never stayed in a hotel in my life, everything in the cabin was novel and exciting. I saw reading lights, night lamps, mirrors on the wall, and a place to hang clothes. I could control the room temperature with a knob and ring a bell to call the attendant. Cabins had no telephones in those days, and we didn't have a balcony either, but we could see the ocean through the porthole.

To my delight, the cabin also had a bathtub, another convenience I was seeing for the first time. I wasted no time in trying it out. I filled it with hot and cold water and poured in bath salts to make bubbles that filled the tub completely. I played with the bubbles and spilled soapy water all over the floor. When I finished and my sister came in, she got quite irritated at the after-effects of my experience.

Under the bed we saw life jackets. We didn't know what they were until we heard a knock on our door. An English gentleman stood there in white shorts and a white shirt with an ID badge on his chest. He identified himself as the purser of the ship and said he was a friend of my father. He had come to escort us to the safety drill on deck. Father had told him that we were traveling alone and didn't speak much English, and asked him to please look after our needs during the four-day voyage. Even though I had finished high school and learned English as a second language, I still found conversation difficult. But we managed to communicate with him in small sentences and with yes or no answers, and we learned that there had been an announcement over the P.A. system, but we hadn't understood it.

We went to the deck with him with our life jackets in our hands and joined the passengers for the drill. They taught us how to put on the jacket and wait for the signal from the crew in the event of evacuation.

As usual, my mind went into overdrive. I remembered the story of how the *Dumra's* sister ship the *S.S. Dara* had sunk in 1961. A bomb had exploded, the ship submerged in flames, and 238 passengers drowned near the coast of Dubai. My parents knew some of the people who died. One of my problems in life is that a story like this becomes a live movie in my mind, and it plays over and over again. Now I started worrying about the minute details of the evacuation procedure. I grew fearful of the turbulence and any unusual movements of the ship. And in fact the sea was a bit rough during the summer months, because of the monsoons, and as we entered the open ocean we felt the boat start to pitch and roll.

When we went back to our cabin we heard a musical bell. I opened the door and saw a man with a xylophone playing a chime repeatedly. I had no idea what it was, but later we learned it was the signal for passengers to go to the mess hall for dinner or lunch.

But a few minutes later, we heard a knock on the door and an attendant came in with a tray full of food. There was biriyani, a delicious spicy rice and meat casserole; nan, a fluffy round bread; and mutton curry. Father had arranged room service for us so we didn't have to go to the mess hall and sit with strangers to eat our meals. From then on, whenever we heard the chimes, we would start salivating as we had a rich, delicious variety of food. These fancy meals with my sister Molly and cousin Alice were enjoyable events. Molly became a little seasick after two days, which was my good fortune. She started eating less and less, and I had no sympathy as I got to eat her portions too!

During the day, we wandered around the deck, watching people sun-bathing and reading, dolphins leaping out of the water and ships passing by. The route to the Persian Gulf was a busy one and the British India Ship Company had many passenger and cargo ships. Occasionally, we ran into the purser. He would ask us how we liked the food and whether we needed anything.

By sundown we retired to our room and waited for dinner to arrive. The assortment of food we had was memorable, and when we reached Muscat we kept asking Ammachy, our mother, to make dishes like we had had on the ship.

On the fourth day we saw Muscat harbor from a distance, and immediately noticed the rocks around the harbor. Ships were unable to dock close to the harbor and anchored a mile away from shore. We started seeing small boats approaching the *Dumra*.

And to my delight, in one boat I saw my father, who was easy to spot because of his full head of white hair. He climbed up a ladder and came onto the deck where we were waiting. He patted my back in greeting, and signaled to the porters to go to our cabin and collect the baggage. He took our passports, as the harbor officials handled the formalities on board. Father seemed to know everyone and soon we were on the small boat heading to shore.

As we neared the dock we saw Ammachy and my brother George, who we called Joychayen, waiting for us. Alice spotted her mother too. Soon we were in our Ammachy's arms. She rolled back my collar, tucked in my shirt, and asked us about the food on the ship and our stay in Bombay. We didn't see Father for a while as he was taking care of the luggage.

From the dock it was just a short walk to our parents' apartment, which had two bedrooms, a living room, a kitchen, and one bathroom. It was on the upper floor of a two-story building with a terrace from which we could see the traffic of the harbor and our ship anchored there. I heard my brother tell my mother that we needed new clothes as the ones we were wearing did not meet his approval. We ate the lunch which Mother had cooked for us. We were so excited at being with our parents that I don't remember what we ate.

Over the holidays, Mother made everything we asked for. Canned food, condensed milk, and cheese were novelties for us. We went to the local markets, which were very smelly and teemed with flies. Mother spoke fluent Arabic and Hindi and bargained with merchants for items like fish and vegetables. Fish were abundant and Mother made fried fish, fish curries, fish biriyani, and fish pickle. Vendors brought vegetables and live chickens to the apartment. That summer holiday, we ate to our hearts' content as Mother made every kind of dish we wished for.

In those days, houses in Muscat had electricity but no running water. People carried water from the interior in leather pouches on the backs of donkeys. We had a regular supplier to bring water for drinking and cooking, and also for bathroom needs. My parents stored it in tanks and used it very carefully. Since we would be living there for two months, Mother ordered two extra bags for the summer.

Electricity was very expensive and our parents could not afford an air conditioning unit. Summer months got very hot and we used to sleep on the terrace at night. Mother sprinkled water on the mattress to cool it. It would quickly evaporate, but some nights we fell asleep immediately during those cool moments.

Father's office was within walking distance and an Indian consulate building stood next to it. As soon as I landed in Muscat, Father realized that my conversational English was inadequate and I lacked the vocabulary expected of a high school graduate. Now that I was facing college admission, he was on my case. The directives were endless. Read the newspaper every day. Write down 10 new words every day. Check them out in a dictionary. Listen to BBC radio for international news. Read *Time*. He took me to different merchants and introduced me to them. He coached me to say, "How do you do?" and to shake hands with strangers and smile at them. He briefed me on how to pay attention to their questions and answer them.

My father had a B.A degree and education was very important to him. He was 5 foot 4 inches tall and always wore white pants and a white shirt. When he went to work outdoors he wore a hard hat and clip-on sunglasses over his spectacles. I realized he had numerous contacts with the local merchants as he was the Lloyd's of London surveyor. He took me to ports where ships unloaded damaged goods and showed me how he assessed the loss in value and wrote reports to the insurance company, giving detailed descriptions of the damage.

Compared to today, Muscat's business center was underdeveloped. There was no delineation between the business and residential areas. There was little traffic, as foreigners could not buy autos and only company cars and taxis traveled the roads.

The harbor was small, horseshoe-shaped, and sheltered from the wind. Muscat was flanked on one side by the ocean and the other by granite mountains. Father used to take me beyond the mountains to the interior in his company jeep. The terrain was miles and miles of endless sand, a desolate landscape broken by occasional green oases owned by wealthy merchants. I saw extensive salt fields as well as orchards, gardens, and palm groves with wells and pumps for watering them.

He took me to petroleum drilling sites, date palm groves, hot springs, and oases in the middle of the desert. He incessantly spoke to me in English. When I replied in Malayalam, he paused to see if I could express the same thought in English. He corrected my vocabulary, grammar, and pronunciation.

He constantly gave me advice about gaining a good education and getting ahead in life. "Don't come to Muscat like me and get stuck in one job," he said repeatedly. "Get a profession and go to England for higher studies." My brother had warned me about my father's desire to see his children well-educated and how he badgered my brother every day as they worked in the same office, correcting his letters and giving him all kinds of advice on the shipping and claim settlements.

Surprisingly, I did not resent his unceasing guidance. I was like a sponge. I hung on to every word and applied all his suggestions. I was very happy that someone was taking an interest in my education. I stored his wise counsel in my mind and I followed through on it during that summer holiday. I wish he had been with me in my childhood to mold me into a better student and person, but destiny did not allow it.

One day he took me to the fort and the big wooden gate that guarded Muscat. It extended across the width of the road that led into the city. The gate was closed at night and the police controlled every car that entered. There was a small arched door open to pedestrians, and Father told me that it was called "eye of the needle" in Arabic. He recounted the parable of Jesus about how it was harder for a rich man to enter the kingdom of God than for a camel to pass through the needle's eye. He explained to me that for a camel to go through the door, the rider would have to dismount and unload all goods on its back. Then the camel would have to crawl through the door and over to the other side. Every time I read that portion in the Bible or whenever I heard a sermon on that topic, I saw my father at the fort standing next to that gate.

During that summer holiday, we took several picnic trips to nearby gardens, beaches, hot water springs, and estates of Father's Arab friends. Father was always lecturing us, but Mother was attentive to all our small needs. She made sure we got new clothes stitched and stocked our school supplies. Occasionally, she splurged on a lavish gift like toys or sports equipment.

My brother George took me to play tennis, badminton, and cricket. He also took me fishing, since the Gulf teemed with fish, and we always returned with a good catch as Brother had honed his skills during his younger days in Mallapally. Father was a good tennis player. He gave me his tennis racket and asked me to join a tennis team when I entered college. He taught me how to fill a college application and to read every line two or three times. He gave me black ballpoint pens, envelopes, and stationery, and asked me to write to him regularly about the colleges I was applying to.

Almost every day we went to the beach, where it was 20 degrees cooler than inside the house. We had to come home before 8 pm as Muscat imposed a curfew at that time for security reasons. Drums beat for 15 minutes before 8 pm to give people in the streets enough time to get indoors. Afterwards, nobody could be out without a lantern. Many houses stocked extra lanterns for friends who needed one to reach home after curfew.

During dinnertime we heard stories from Mother about our toddler days and the Arab lady Sarah who had looked after my sister and me. One day Sarah showed up at our house. She was ecstatic to see how grown up we were and started chattering to my mother nonstop in Arabic. It was obvious she was very happy to see us and she gave my sister and me big bear hugs. Sarah told us how she used to sit on the floor with her knees in the lotus position and rock my sister and me on both knees. She fed us and put us to sleep as Mother's health was not good those days.

The days passed very quickly and soon the summer holidays came to an end. With reluctant hearts and teary eyes we said good-bye to our parents, knowing that we would not see them again for another three long years.

As I stood on the deck and watched Muscat harbor dwindle in the distance, my mind started reliving the summer spent with my parents. It was the most memorable time I had ever had with them. On other occasions, it was Mother who came to India to settle us in a new school or arrange my brothers' marriages, or Father who arrived for vacation but got busy building our new house in Tiruvalla. When he was in town, family members and visitors also flooded our home and took up his time.

But during this vacation, I saw my father in his workplace. I saw his great discipline and daily routine, and his sincerity at work and in dealing with his clients. I also saw how he lived an honorable, principled life. I realized how loyal and devoted he was to his family, and how much he wanted his children to study well and achieve something. I saw the moral and honest life he led amid opportunities to act otherwise. As a surveyor for an insurance company, he could have accepted the bribes that wealthy merchants offered him to inflate the damages for their claims. My brother George, who continues to work in the insurance business in Muscat, testifies that 35 years later people still recall and revere Father's integrity.

During that summer, I clearly realized that he had a dream about me. A seed of hope was planted in me that if I studied hard, I could live up to his dreams. This became a driving force in my life. I felt enriched and enlightened by this visit with my parents, and I felt confident that with education I was on the avenue to success.

CHAPTER 12

In the Newspaper

My name appeared in a newspaper for the first time on May 21, 1967. My neighbor shouted this fact across the fence to my mother. I was 17 and I had gone for my medical school interview in Davangere, near Bangalore. I was expected back by train from Bangalore, but this article arrived before I did.

The railways are the spine of Indian economy, as the trucking industry is in the United States. They networked almost all cities and train travel was affordable to average citizens. The privileged ones traveled in first class and reserved compartments. This system had a big impact in my life, as the trains have taken me to many parts of India.

After a long day of travel back from medical school, returning with my cousin and uncle, I had reached Bangalore. It was a cosmopolitan city even then, and its railway station was unlike anything familiar to citizens of the United States. In fact, it was a microcosm of the world beyond.

The platform had waiting rooms for the upper-class travelers and nice restaurants for those who could afford them. But most travelers depended on the vendors or brought their own food for the journey.

Vendors were everywhere. They had to sell their goods before the train left in order to make a meager profit and put food on their tables. So even though their prices were rock-bottom, passengers bargained with them until they were desperate. I saw strolling vendors selling finger foods: banana chips, bananas fried in a batter, fried onions, fried potatoes, peanuts wrapped in newspaper, peanut brittle, chocolates, cookies. Tea and coffee were available from licensed vendors as well as the street boys who walked around selling these beverages from nearby restaurants for a meager commission. There were no CDs, iPods, or MP3 players in those days, but the magazine and newspaper booths were very busy as people bought reading material for the train. I saw balloons, toys, and items to amuse travelers during the trip. From behind the iron fences, people tried to sell products of the small-scale industry they operated, like baskets, coir (coconut fiber rope) mattresses, and pillows. These goods were not travel-related and vendors had trouble getting a license to sell them on the platform. I saw palm readers with one eye on the outstretched hand and the other on the horizon in case policemen were coming to evict them. You name it and people were selling it. All you had to do was to tune into their chants and voices to hear their wares.

Beggars crowded the railway station. Scrawny children held out their hands in the universal plea for food or money. Mothers in tattered saris carried naked babies with runny noses. Some resourceful and relatively healthy beggars caught your attention by singing to the drumbeat of their palms on their concave, malnourished stomachs. Most people, including me, ignored them, as they were such a common sight. The mind becomes numb to the extreme poverty that surrounds you.

I also heard people shouting at the top of their voices, calling to friends or family to position themselves so when the train arrived they could get a seat without running anxiously up and down the platform looking for empty spaces. They spoke in a babel of tongues, as passengers came from different south Indian states. India is a land of 16 major languages as diverse as English and German. Despite the hubbub, I saw people sleeping on the floor while waiting for the next train.

I remember a group of nuns that day — six of them sitting on the platform, minding their own business and ignoring the drama of human interaction and the people deploying the skillful strategies needed for a train journey in India. By these, I mean timing your arrival at the platform, assessing where the open compartments would be, aligning yourself to them, and elbowing your way into the train before it completely stopped. If you paid the porter, he would go inside, spread his turban on the seat, and hold it for you as you strolled leisurely inside.

Much of this vivid scene is now history. Train travel in India today is much better organized and you can make reservations online. You hear announcements on the loudspeaker about arriving trains and the platform numbers for departing ones. You can sit in air-conditioned coaches, and sleep in comfortable berths over long distances. But the clamor of the old railway stations became deeply etched in my memory as I traveled back and forth from medical school to my home for my semester breaks during the next five years.

Eventually I heard my train rumbling in. Its engine blasted steam and the driver pulled the shrieking whistle to alert careless pedestrians crossing the track. The noise on the platform rose to a higher pitch as everyone started chattering and yelling to family members, "Move here!" "Over there! "Jump in now!" "Get out!" A few porters shouted that the baggage was very heavy and they needed extra money. Since clean drinking water was not available, the vendors' cries grew louder as they tried to sell coffee and tea to last-minute customers.

Sometimes the vendors leaped onto the train illegally, but it didn't happen that day, since the train was loaded beyond full capacity with passengers and luggage. I went inside. People were standing in the corridors so there was no room for anyone to move around, and many were cooling themselves with hand-held fans. Luggage was piled up on the upper berths and all over the floor, wherever there was space.

I managed to find a seat, so I knew I could sleep after a while. Exhaustion from the full day of travel caught up with me and the summer heat put me in a stupor. There was also a small noisy fan, not strong enough to actually move the air, but loud enough to lull you into slumber. Sleep was the only way to escape the discomfort of sitting on a hard wooden bench until I reached my destination.

At 6:10 pm. I heard the double bell and the whistle from the driver, and I knew we were leaving the station on time. Like most passenger trains, ours started at very slowly until the caboose cleared the platform. There was a last-minute rush of people trying to get in and vendors leaping off the rolling cars.

As the train moved out of the platform it picked up speed and generated a breeze, and people dropped their fans. Many passengers had been waiting hours to find a place to rest inside the train. Now they took out their prepared meals and start eating. Playing cards was normally a good way to pass the time, and on most journeys people could use a suitcase or trunk as a card table, but this train was so overcrowded they had no room to move around or stretch.

The sounds inside the compartment differed from those on the platform. They came from human chatter. Some people were discussing family matters, others complaining about the trouble they had during the previous leg of the journey, and still others bragging about their jobs. Conversations usually took place between families and friends, but it was not impolite for others to join in. I rarely heard formal introductions between passengers, and sometimes a stranger would respond after a person had tossed out a question or made a statement. Always in the background I heard the sound of the wheels clicking on the railway tracks: *tuck-tuck, tuck-tuck, tuck-tuck.* It created a rhythm like a lullaby.

One of the comforts I enjoyed during my train journey was the light in the compartment, which made it possible to read even at night. Many people read on the train since they knew the electric power wouldn't fail. In the outside world, unpredictable blackouts were common. You'd sit down for dinner and the power would go out. Then someone had to light a candle or a lamp for everyone to finish eating and clean up. Or you'd sit down to study and the power would go out. Then you'd have to depend on lanterns or candles to keep reading until the power came back on. Or you'd start to shower and the power would go off, and you'd have to use your non-visual senses to exit the bathroom safely. In your own home you could manage fairly well, but it was more challenging if you were at someone else's house. There was much unpredictability about electricity in daily life, but the train had a generator and the compartment had a bright light. Unlike the reserved sleeping first-class compartments, in third class there was a no lights-off policy. You could sink into a book for as long as you wanted.

It was past 9 pm. The passengers were quiet and many of them were reading. The lucky ones had found a seat on the wooden bench, leaning against the window. Many others sat on the floor or stood grasping the overhead straps, swaying to the rhythm of the train.

The train's *tuck-tuck* had picked up a rapid rhythm. I was just starting to close my eyes and nod off. We had passed the town of Kuppam, which is famous for its granite quarries, and one variety of granite bears the name of the town: Kuppam Green.

Suddenly the lights went off and the smooth momentum of the train changed to jerks. I saw that the train was leaning to the side. We rolled three times and the passengers and luggage inside the compartment tumbled together like scrambled eggs. In the pitch dark all you could hear was screaming and crying. I heard the names of gods of every religion and people screamed out for their loved ones.

I wanted to call out the names of my cousin and uncle, but no voice came out of my throat. I felt like the air had been sucked out of my lungs. I realized that I was upside down under the seat, squeezed in between luggage and people. Occasionally the car jerked as people tried to move or get out of the train.

My struggle to breathe became harder as the weight of the luggage and people crushing me almost choked me to death. I prayed silently and asked God to help me escape. I must be one of few people who have ever prayed to God to spare my life while hanging upside down! Later it became a family joke that God answered if you prayed upside down.

After an hour and a half I started feeling that I could move my elbows as people were trying to clear the luggage, human bodies, and body parts around me. Guided by the noise I crawled toward the window and writhed out of the train with the help of fellow passengers and the crowd that had gathered from the surrounding neighborhood.

It was around 10 pm and I could see a lot of people in the darkness. My rail-car had become detached from the main train, which was still on the track, and it had landed at the bottom of an embankment. There was total chaos on the ground as there were no emergency response teams in those days. Aid came from other passengers who were willing to help the people inside that mangled compartment and to face the horrible smell of blood and human beings trapped within.

I sat on the ground and felt my forehead. I realized that I was bleeding profusely and staunched the blood by pressing on it with my hand. A few people had flashlights and the able-bodied walked around to see who needed help. People were still screaming and calling for their friends and relatives. I was numb and frightened and made no attempt to scream, but tried to locate my cousin's voice. I felt heaviness in my chest and became short of breath. When I coughed, I tasted blood.

A good Samaritan tore his white *mundu* and made a bandage to stop my bleeding. I sat on the ground trembling and watched the chaos, not knowing what to do next. I tried to check the time and realized that my watch had broken off from my wrist.

Then I heard my cousin Geekkutty's voice calling his father, "Papa, papa!" In the pitch darkness with a few candles and cigarette lighters turning on and off, it was impossible to locate him. I did not have the strength to run toward that voice as I was struggling to breathe and blood had soaked my bandage. I was consoled by the thought that someone I knew was alive and I would get help soon.

Suddenly I saw my cousin. He said my uncle was safe but had a rip in his earlobe which was bleeding badly. We walked over to him. I don't know how much time passed but we were happy that we were together.

By this time a newspaper reporter came by and took our names and another person came and asked us whether we needed to send any messages home. My uncle gave him some money and asked him to send a telegram to his house saying that all three of us were safe. Later we found out that the telegram never got there.

At about 3 am the medical train arrived from the nearest city, Perambur. It was a moving hospital with all the facilities: nurses, doctors, cast room, and even an operating theater. It had floodlights to illuminate the accident scene. They took us onto the train and I got immediate treatment as my forehead was bleeding a lot. After putting stitches on my wound they kept me in a bed on the train.

The rescue team worked until dawn attending to all the wounded passengers. When the sun came out we saw dead bodies lined up on the ground. We were told they removed 125 bodies from our train car. That memory is hard for me to shake even today. Almost everyone I had seen earlier in the compartment had died. We were among the lucky 25 who survived.

The medical train rolled away and headed to Perambur, in Madras state, which had one of the best railway hospitals in southern India. Established in 1928, it had specialties in surgery, gynecology, and pediatrics even in its early years.

Every part of my body hurt and I experienced shooting pain when I took a deep breath. They found me a bed in a long ward with 25 to 30 patients lined up on either side. Each patient's chart hung on a metal clipboard at the foot of the bed. No curtains or walls separated the beds, and when a patient needed a private examination they rolled a portable screen to the bedside. Two or three fans hung from the high ceiling and rotated, but I felt no air movement.

Patient-watching was a good way to pass the time for those who could lift their heads off the pillow. The ward could get very noisy as every patient had one or two family members who spoke not only to their loved one but to anyone who had anything in common to talk about. You would hear at least three or four languages in a regional hospital like this. People who spoke the same tongue have a common bond and I saw relatives comparing notes with their newfound friends.

I remember seeing the doctor and the nurses appear at the entrance of the ward. During those days, doctors in India always wore pants and shirt while the rest of the population wore their traditional *dhothi*, a six-foot long white cloth wrapped around the waist in a style that varied with the region. I was awed by their white coats and the stethoscopes hanging from their necks. I was impressed by the confidence with which they walked around the hospital. I watched their every move, imagining that one day I might also walk and talk like them.

When the doctor entered the ward, the noise level dropped and patients and relatives waited for their turn for him to come to their bedside. The doctor would talk to patients, turn to the nurse, and speak in English using medical jargon nobody grasped. The nurse would nod and seem to understand. An orderly walked behind him carrying a basin half full of disinfectant water. The doctor would dip his hands in the basin and wipe his hands on a towel hanging from the orderly's hand. I saw the doctor tapping patients' chests and listening to their hearts and lungs with his stethoscope. What he heard through that stethoscope was a big mystery for me until I entered medical school.

Placing a stethoscope around my neck had been a childhood dream of mine. I had seen Dr. George, our family physician, walking around the hospital with his stethoscope. My mother took me to him when I got a cold or chest infection. He would open my mouth and look inside, and then listen to my chest through that tube. I was curious about what he was hearing. I had seen the missionary Dr. Davis, who walked the corridors holding that tube like a rabbit with two legs hanging at the end. I had seen Dr. Lilly, the pediatrician, dangling that tube in front of the babies when she talked to mothers, as the babies tried to catch it. I had seen Dr. John at my father's bedside with the tube sticking from his coat pocket like two eyes bulging out. I had seen Dr. Mathew with the stethoscope thrown over his left shoulder and clinging to his neck like a towel. I had noticed that anybody with that tube received instant recognition inside and outside a hospital and I wanted it too.

When the ward doctor reached me, he asked the nurse to remove the bandage around my head and he checked for signs of infection or bleeding. He pressed the six-inch gash over my right eyebrow. I had no sensation there. He explained that a nerve was cut and that the right side of my scalp would be numb for a long time. He listened to my lungs and heart, and asked the nurse to arrange for another chest X-ray and to have me see a lung specialist. He suspected rib fractures and a bruised lung, and he told her to give me extra medication for my pain.

The doctor moved on to the next patient and I studied his interactions with each patient. Even though the pain from the trauma was intense, the hope that one day I would walk around in a hospital ward helping in suffering eased my agony. I started to understand a patient's yearning for the doctor's reassuring words in even the worst circumstances. Watching the bustle of the hospital routine put me in a state of trance as I dreamed of the day when I would be on the other side of the stethoscope.

Back home, my terrified mother woke up my older brother George and told him that the train I was traveling in had had an accident and that my name was on the injured list in the newspaper. George consoled her, packed a small bag, and headed off. At Ernakulum station he met one of our relatives and borrowed some money as he did not know the extent of my injuries. The railway bulletin board listed my name under persons with head injuries.

When he reached the accident scene, an official said all head injury patients were dead and that my brother could look through the dead bodies to try to identify me. I had a deviated right toe and thick hair like him so he summoned the courage to look through the bodies. He later told our family it was the most traumatic experience in his life.

Later, officials directed him to the railway hospital. I remember him walking into our ward with tears of joy running down his face and an expression of relief beyond description that I was still alive and able to walk up to him and hug him. We hugged so tight that I almost stopped breathing because of my lung contusion, but our emotions were so intense that we both cry even today when we recall that moment.

He looked at the big linen wrapping on my forehead, and examined my hands and legs to make sure that no limbs were missing, since he had seen body parts at the accident scene. He did not speak much for awhile as he was still in shock and we stared at each other silently thanking God for His mercy.

That same day my maternal grandfather P.I. Joseph, my cousin Dr. Grace John (Njolma), then a medical student at Mangalore, and my uncle E.V. Paily came to the hospital. Even though I was in much pain and breathing shallowly, a sense of security seeped into me with the assurance that my grandfather and my brother would take care of everything.

The next day the Indian railway minister arrived at the hospital to visit the injured passengers. To see a minister up close is a big event in India, especially when one arrives with security guards, assistant secretaries, and the press. I saw him shaking hands with patients in the rows in our ward.

When he reached me, someone told him that I was going to go to medical school. He said, "You now have firsthand experience of being a patient and seeing how hospitals function — even before you start medical school." I was tongue-tied so I smiled as I stood there looking at him and his entourage. But I grew excited that I would soon be learning to ease suffering, and his words rang in my ears for many years to come. He told his secretary to give me 250 rupees for incidental expenses and moved on to the next patient. His secretary arranged tickets for all of us to return home.

Overall, we received excellent medical care at this hospital (and free railway fare for any family members who wanted to visit us). In the end, after the X-rays and consultation with the pulmonologist, I was assured that I had no broken ribs and that the lung contusion would heal in its own time. I spit up blood for three weeks.

CHAPTER 13

"Butcher, Butcher!"

I started medical college in 1968, when I was 18. I was enthusiastic about it in many ways, but fearful of the hard work ahead. I was attending a school in the state of Karnataka where the local language, Kannada, was foreign to me. Fortunately, two senior students from Kerala were already there. They had found a place to stay and asked me to join them. It was a Church of South India (CSI) compound in a beautiful spot in the middle of Davangere, full of eucalyptus and neem trees. The pastor was a sweet young man who liked to have budding doctors and engineers around, so he let students stay in a building on the church grounds free of charge. It had a central hall with two dormitory-like rooms on either side, one for medical students and the other for engineering students. Each of us had just a cot and a shared bathroom. There was no kitchen.

I had studied in Malayalam until I finished high school. Now, my medium of instruction was English. I had learned it as a second language, so I could read and write it. However, I had a limited grasp of it and I was not comfortable speaking in English. Imagine learning everything in your native language till you entered college and then having to study medical science with all its special terms in a different tongue. Indian languages were not that difficult for me, and I can speak four of them, but English bears little resemblance to them and grasping everything in English was a real challenge. Moreover, I not only had to master English but also all the terminology of Latin and other languages from which many medical terms are derived.

After the first anatomy lecture, I had a headache trying to digest what the teacher was explaining. He held a thighbone in one hand and told us it was called a femur. It was the longest bone in the body. The vastus medialis muscle originated in the femoral neck and was inserted into the tibial tubercle. The bone's nutrient blood vessel was the femoral artery. The tensor fascia lata ligament supported the femur and the structures attached. The femoral head was inserted into the acetabulum. As I came out of the lecture hall I heard the senior students talking about foramen rotundum, medulla oblongata, posterior cerebellar artery, and coracoids process. Wow! What had I signed up for? Was this even English or was it some utterly alien language?

I went back to my room and opened Gray's *Anatomy*, my textbook, which was three times bigger than my Bible. The terminology was extremely complicated and I struggled to pronounce the Latin words. Where did I start and how could I get a handle on these strange terms? I was petrified of the task ahead, but I had no choice. I could not disappoint my father who had invested so much hope and money in my future career.

Help came from senior students. One of them advised me to buy a medical dictionary and an English dictionary. Painstakingly, I read and reread the anatomy textbook. Slowly, I started understanding the terms.

The next challenge was to remember and recall them. I realized this task was crucial. Help came from a *Reader's Digest* ad I spotted for memory training by Harry Lorayne. I used visualization, association, and mnemonic devices to sharpen my memory. With the help of these three aids, I started my battle with the medical curriculum.

The first major hurdle was to overcome the queasiness of entering the anatomy dissection hall. I knew that I would be spending a year and half there, dissecting a whole human body and learning the details of every muscle, artery, nerve, and organ.

The smell of formalin welcomed us into the anatomy hall, as its attendant had taken all the cadavers out of the formalin tank and placed them on the dissecting tables. My eyes started tearing from the formalin fumes and I approached a table that had a dissection box with scalpel, scissors, forceps, and probe.

We were assigned in sets of four to dissect the hands, legs, and face. The dissection manual had step-by-step instructions for dissecting each part, but nobody wanted to begin until the anatomy tutor showed up next to our table. He taught us the basic principles: how to make the skin incision, turn back the skin to expose the muscles, and keep each exposed part moist with formalin towels.

With shaky hands, I ventured to dissect the palm of the hand. The skin was tough and I had no idea how deep to go until I reached the inside structures. I followed the manual and thought I had exposed the small muscles of the hand reasonably well.

Suddenly a hush fell over the hall and we saw our anatomy professor, Dr. Sheriff, walking in. He was a real taskmaster and everyone grew anxious around him as he was a perfectionist and expected his students to be as well. He always wore a white shirt and white pants, and prowled around the dissection hall with his probe in the hand. He had very thick glasses and his piercing stare made students extremely nervous when he approached their table. Although we focused on the dissection, we always kept him in our peripheral vision, wondering when he would loom over us.

Like a predator stalking its prey, he came to our table. He asked our names and examined our work. Suddenly he grabbed the forceps from me, pulled a small piece of the muscle attached to the skin of the palm I had dissected, and asked me what it was. I said it was the palmaris brevis muscle. He asked why it was attached to the skin but not the bone. I explained that by accident I had cut deeper than I thought and the muscle had become detached from the bone.

"Butcher, butcher!" he bellowed so loudly that the other students froze and stared at our table.

My whole body started shaking. I was speechless and stood there like a stunned animal. I don't remember anything he said after that. I wanted to crawl under the desk and disappear. At the end of that session I cried all the way back to my room. I crashed onto my bed and slept out of exhaustion and confusion.

The slight breeze through the window woke me up. The aroma of eucalyptus trees filled the room. I got up and took a walk outside. The gentle breeze made the eucalyptus trees flutter and filled the air with a pleasant scent. It was just the calm my bruised ego needed.

Yet I started questioning my ability to continue in medical school. Did I have the brainpower to tackle the challenges ahead? Should I pack up and go home, and tell my parents that I was sorry but I was not fit for this profession? I recalled my father's look when he saw me off at the railway station. I saw the pride and hope in his face and I didn't know how he could bear it if I gave up. No one in my house had ever attended a professional college. Father was ecstatic at the thought of my becoming a doctor and bringing distinction to our family.

I wanted to go to the pastor's house and confess my decision to give up. I recalled his genial face and the warmth with which he had offered room and board for the five medical and three engineering students whom he was shepherding forward toward our dreams.

I stared over the compound wall and watched the people pass by. Many were going to the nearby movie theater. Some were returning from offices and a few were carrying shopping bags. Many peasants walked barefoot with all their belongings on their back. I tried to listen in on their conversations, but they were speaking in a different language. Their poverty was obvious from their garb.

My mind started to ask the right questions. Why was I here? Getting the best education would change my future and guarantee a decent life. I would become a valuable, useful person to society.

I heard the music over the loudspeaker from the movie theater signaling that the next show was about to begin. I returned to my room and saw my roommates poring over their books. Without disturbing them, I sat on my bed, pulled the dissection manual from the window shelf, and started reading. I don't think I grasped much that day but I sat with the book in my lap until physical and mental exhaustion forced me to turn off the bedside lamp and go to sleep.

At 4:30 a.m., I woke up to the gushing sound of water from the bathroom. The city water supply was available only from 4:30 to 5:30, and we had to collect the water at that time in big vessels for our daily needs. The lecture started at 7:30 am. We mounted our bicycles and pedaled the two miles to college.

The first hour was physiology. Dr. Sengupta introduced himself as the professor and head of the physiology department. He wore a suit and tie, and had a wooden pointer almost as long as a pole that he leaned on during the lecture. He paced from side to side on the stage explaining how the kidneys filtered urine from the blood. His accent needed getting used to. He pronounced urine as "uryne." The class giggled for a while but his lecture was interesting so the students learned to focus on the substance and got used to his accent. He was a soft-spoken, gentle man and made everyone comfortable. He reassured us that he would make physiology interesting. I felt a little light of hope inside that if I hung on I might make it.

My legs were hesitant to take me back to the anatomy hall that day, fearing that I would once again be the target of Dr. Sheriff's wrath. On that day, Dr. Naik, the anatomy tutor, was in charge. He was tall, slim, and dapper in his fancy shirt and tie. He spoke articulately and explained the methodology for studying anatomy. He made us comfortable and told us that Dr. Sheriff was strict but that by the end of the year we would all have benefited from his thoroughness. Today I realize that Dr. Sheriff was training us to be absolutely meticulous when we dissected, even with a cadaver. In a few years, we would be operating on live human bodies and we would have no room for error.

I liked Dr. Naik from the very first day. All through my anatomy studies I gravitated towards him for advice. I sat on the front bench for all his lectures. He was very popular among the students as his teaching style was engaging and he was friendly to us outside the lecture hall. I studied anatomy so intensely that on the final exam I scored first in the class. This mark greatly boosted my confidence.

Finally, I cleared the basic anatomy and physiology classes, which earned me the privilege of hanging a stethoscope around my neck, and I never lost my enthusiasm for it all through my career. Every day when I picked up that instrument, I thanked God for that privilege, and prayed that I would hear the right sounds to make the correct diagnosis for each patient I encountered. I never dreamt that a day would come when I would be on the other side of the stethoscope.

Chapter 14

Through Medical School and India

Important people surrounded me in medical school and helped ease the journey. One was Bhaskaran, my childhood servant who came to stay with me and cook for me all through these years. At 4.30 in the morning, he would tap me on my leg to wake me up. He would hold a cup of black coffee for me in one hand and an unlit cigarette for himself in the other. If I were in a deep sleep, he would go outside and smoke his cigarette, heat up the coffee again after 15 minutes, and come back. Later, after I returned from classes, I always took a nap. Bhaskaran would wake me for dinner after which I'd stay up late into the night studying. This was my daily routine.

Bhaskaran knew my parents' yearning to see me succeed. And by sending Bhaskaran with me, they made sure that I wouldn't have to worry about cooking or maintaining a house. I shared the house with four other students, since dorm life was unsupervised and my parents worried about drinking in student residences. The newspapers also occasionally ran horror stories about extreme hazing.

Bhaskaran cleaned the house, did all the grocery shopping, and looked after all of us like an older brother. Since he knew me from birth, we had an unusual bond, and his loyalty was unmatched. He was our watchman, our cook, and our guardian. Above all, he was the friendly face that greeted us with a cup of coffee and a snack after our hectic hospital rounds and classes, and listened to the joys or sorrows of our day. Sometimes he reminded me of childhood events such as at age five, I threw a tantrum in the marketplace because he wouldn't take me to see a juggler or the times I fought with him about going to the barbershop. He used to brush away the hair clippings from my face with his hand towel because they bothered me.

I shared my dreams with him and told him that when I became a doctor, I would buy a car and drive him around. I promised to take him shopping for new clothes. I told him that I would get on an airplane and go to England. When I came back, I would speak with an accent like an English gentleman and have lots of money in my pocket. He used to say, "When you come back, I will come and see you. I will put my hand in your pocket and take as much money as I want." Within seven years I was able to fulfill his dream. Even though distance separates us now, our bond is still alive and strong. At boarding school, I often felt despondent and homesick. In medical school I rarely did, because of Bhaskaran.

The presence of my cousin Geekutty also greatly helped. He had survived the train wreck with me and lived in the same house. We ate together, studied together, and traveled back and forth together from medical school to our homes during vacation. Whenever we passed the accident scene, our antennae went up. We listened to every sound the train made and we looked at each other, silently acknowledging that things would be all right this time. Whenever I became discouraged, he cheered me up and refocused me. He reminded me not to waste my precious time worrying about mundane things.

Friends can make your college days happy and productive. My immediate circle comprised the students who shared the house with me. Two of them, Raju and Rajan, were senior students and our role models. I watched what they studied and focused on how they managed the difficult portions. I always asked their advice about the classes I was going to take. Rajan and I shared a room separated by a cardboard screen to keep the glare of our table lamps from each other's faces. We respected each other's schedules and fostered a good studying atmosphere.

I noticed Sethu Madhavan during my first year. He always sat in front of the class, and at the end of the lecture he usually asked very interesting questions. Sethu came from the neighboring state of Madras. Since the college had students from many states in India, during the first year people gravitated to others from their own state who spoke the same language.

I became friends with Sethu after the first-year exam, as we were among the top five students in the class. Indeed, he was my best friend all through medical school, and even today. We started sharing ideas and comparing notes. We discussed pathology and pharmacology in our spare time. This friendship grew into a healthy competition, and I watched carefully to see what books he read, how he wrote his notes, and how many hours he studied. Sethu lived in the dorm and I stayed in a house across from him, but we could see the lights from our rooms. When I grew weary of studying at 2 a.m., I would look out the window. If Sethu's light was still on, I would study one more chapter to make sure that I didn't lag behind.

We spent many hours together in the library and we often sat on the steps of the verandah studying difficult topics. We analyzed our study strategies during coffee breaks and any spare moments, discussing how to optimize our efforts and get the best results. We prioritized the chapters we needed to spend more time on. We tried to predict which questions would appear on the exam. Sethu enjoyed Bhaskaran's cooking while we studied the citric acid cycle and pathology of inflammation. We often bicycled to interesting places and went on picnics and hikes. We shared our hopes about our future wives. We dreamed about our final exam. I encouraged his ambition to become the gold medalist in the university. We imagined coming to America together, and planned our timing of the eligibility exam for the U.S. visa soon after graduation. Fifteen years later, Sethu would be instrumental in helping me fulfill my dream by sponsoring me to work in the United States.

There were no distractions like parties among any of us, as we all had the same goal. The television era had not begun in India, and the transistor radio on Geekuttychayan's desk was the sole entertainment I can recall. But I remember the day Neil Armstrong landed on the moon. We kept our ears glued to the radio in the middle of the night. Our only guilty pleasures were a movie once or twice a month, a visit to a café for a coffee, and a snack which might cost just a few coins. Even though we were at an age when hormones were rampant, the watchful eyes of society and the segregation of sexes in classrooms, churches, and all public places kept us from teenage temptations.

The college did organize a few field trips and excursions, and the most memorable was the All-India Tour with 50 other classmates. Our principal Gurupadappa said, "You are a bunch of nerds. It's time that you got out of this city and saw the rest of India." He offered us use of the new college bus. We would share the cost of gas and drivers' pay, and we had a class-mate, the son of a successful businessman, who was ready and willing to manage the trip.

But first we had to get through our fourth-year final exams, among the toughest in the curriculum. We had to pass pathology, forensic medicine, ophthalmology, and preventive medicine to make it to the last year, in which we would practice clinical medicine.

On the day after our last test, at 4 am on a cold January day, we loaded our luggage onto the bus and set off on the trip of a lifetime. Our principal came to wish us good luck and Dr. Naik, who was leaving for the United States, told us to contact him if we needed help. Sethu was my seatmate for the whole 21-day trip.

Our first stop was Bombay, the financial center of India. We were excited to see Malabar Hill, the Beverly Hills of Bombay, and beautiful Juhu Beach. Since my uncle lived in Bombay, I took a train and visited him, joining the tour the next day.

We saw Trombay, the atomic energy center where the scientific brain-power of India was concentrated. The director of the plant gave us a guided tour. Through the observation glass, we saw people wearing astronaut-like suits working on the plutonium plant.

Then we traveled further through northern India, an area magical to someone who grew up in the south. You see the history left behind by

British rule, the government buildings in the capital city Delhi, and the splendor of majestic mountains in Simla, Kashmir, and Darjeeling.

Snow had blocked the road to Kashmir and buses could not get through. But our tour leader convinced the Indian Airlines office to charter a plane for us so that we wouldn't miss its beauty. We flew to Srinagar, the capital of Kashmir, and as we descended, I saw a blanket of white. Snow! I was seeing it for the first time in my life. As soon as we got onto the tarmac, we started throwing snowballs at each other until the security guard escorted us to the waiting bus. None of us had the right winter clothing for Kashmir, but our joy at seeing snow kept our adrenaline high and probably helped keep us warm.

We stayed on a houseboat in Dal Lake, the most picturesque part of Kashmir, which most Indians see only in movies. The houseboat was comfortable but had no heating. We shivered the whole night until we could shower the next day with one bucket of hot water each. We saw beautiful Gulmarg Park and other tourist attractions commonly shown on calendars and postcards. Kashmiri women are famous for their beauty and fair complexions. We glanced at them surreptitiously and savored their loveliness.

We took a flight back to Delhi, where the bus and drivers waited for us. We stayed in a *satram*, a traveler's inn run by the Hindu Society, for a cheap rate and relished the hot water at only fifty paisa per bucket. There, on January 26, we experienced the highlight of our trip: the Republic Day Parade. Republic Day commemorates the adoption of India's constitution and freedom from British rule. The sight of fighter planes in formation and the armed forces on parade was unforgettable.

The Taj Mahal was the next stop. We were eager to see this famous attraction. The Mughal emperor Shajahan built it as a tomb for his beloved wife Mumtaz, and Rabindranath Tagore, India's Nobel laureate for literature, reputedly described it as a marvel in marble, a wonder in stone, and a tear on the cheek of time. Indeed, the sight of it takes your breath away and makes you speculate whether this astonishing memorial was really man-made at a time when there were no cranes or proper transportation to bring the marble and all the precious stones needed to build it.

Our journey veered north again to explore the neighboring country of Nepal. The Pashupathy temple was legendary and famous for its many hippie tourists in those days. Some students wanted to try LSD. It was the sixties, after all! Others wandered around the city looking for nightclubs, which are few and far between in India. I bought some foreign clothes and a small transistor radio.

We then continued on to visit Calcutta, Hyderabad, and Simla. The trip took just three weeks but the memories have lasted me a lifetime and the education, the exposure to my native land, was invaluable.

CHAPTER 15

Becoming a Doctor

I t was during the fifth and final year of medical school that I felt the emotional flip. I grew up as a timid child. Some members of my family doubted that I would finish medical school and I myself felt I was struggling, working hard to realize the impossible. Fear and worry controlled my life until then, but as I saw myself finishing the final exam without much difficulty, I realized that hope was erasing my negative emotions.

I felt a restlessness creeping into me to show my family and friends that I could become a full-fledged physician. The anatomy of the facial nerve that I studied in the first year helped me talk to a patient with facial nerve palsy and reassure him that it would not affect his eyes since different nerves controlled them. The study of liver physiology helped me diagnose a hepatitis patient and monitor the enzymes to predict the course of the disease. The blood chemistry I studied in the first year proved handy when I came across patients with anemia and leukemia. The fetal development studies in my second year made me marvel when I delivered my first baby. The pharmacology and metabolism of various medications I studied in the third year helped me prescribe the right antibiotic when seeing patients with pneumonia. The pathology lecture slides of leukemia and lymphoma I studied in fourth year gave me insight into cell biology and the prognosis of cancer patients. The microbiology of tuberculosis and its devastating effect on human body became real when I started seeing patients emaciated with the disease and spitting up blood when they coughed. The ferocity of the leprosy bacteria that can eat away the nose and fingers made me realize that the colorful slides we had seen through the microscope in the pathology lab had profound clinical implications. The glucose metabolism studied in physiology now helped me to control sugar in diabetic patients. The normal vital signs I learned in anatomy and physiology class helped me spot abnormal patterns that needed interpretation. I had daily reminders that smoking, considered cool, shriveled the lungs and made you gasp when doing simple chores. I saw cirrhosis of the liver caused by alcohol consumption that made the belly fill with fluid. The mystery of the appendix struck me when a patient came in with abdominal pain and had to be taken to the operating room for immediate removal of that organ. But the magic of surgery with its swift cures in the OR especially attracted me, and I decided to become a surgeon.

On the day when I went in for the final exam, I followed my ritual of carrying the plastic ruler my father had given me, which had "British India Shipping Co." printed on it in red letters, and the lucky pen that I would use from high school through completing my postgraduate FRCP (that is, Fellow of the Royal College of Physicians) examination in Canada.

Afterwards, my shoulders felt the relief that I no longer had to sit in front of the books for hours and hours. After a two-week break, I started my internship at the hospital affiliated with my medical school.

My first posting was pediatrics. During the second week, we had to go to a nearby village for a mass immunization. Two interns, four nurses, and an orderly set up the booths and gave the vaccinations. It was heartbreaking to see children roaming around not knowing where their next meal was coming from, but I felt satisfaction that with our polio and MMR vaccines we could at least keep them from getting preventable diseases. The day went very well and we immunized more than 50 children in the neighborhood and its nearby villages.

When we returned to the hospital, I stepped out of the van and tripped. I landed on my right hand and immediately realized I had fractured my wrist. An X-ray confirmed it. My orthopedic professor Dr. Shetty reduced my fracture and put on a cast.

Life came to a halt. Since I had injured my right hand, I couldn't use a stethoscope, I couldn't pump the blood pressure machine, and I couldn't write patient notes and prescriptions. My timetable for the different rotations was now meaningless. The cast wouldn't come off for six weeks, and I had no idea how much time I would need to build up my strength and be functional again. I was filled with frustration and disappointment. My classmates would get ahead of me and I chafed at being left behind.

I reluctantly said good-bye to the city where I had lived as a medical student for five years, and returned home to recover. It was a sobering moment for my parents as they had been ecstatic about my progress. I had told them about my ambition to go to the United States for higher studies, but now the clock had stopped and the only significant event before me was the removal of the cast and the return of function to my hand. But mothers are at their best when their children ail, and I basked in my mother's pampering.

The cast came off after six weeks and the follow-up X-ray showed that the fracture was over-reduced. I would be unable to do certain simple movements like tightening a light bulb or rotating my wrist. My ambition to become a surgeon was shattered and the coin flipped. I learned the life lesson that being a doctor does not guarantee protection from accidents and disease.

I decided to apply for an internship in my home state of Kerala and started training at Trivandrum Medical College. In May, 1975, I fulfilled the dream I had harbored since I was five years old. I received my medical degree.

Looking back, I am convinced that my rigorous training and excellent teachers prepared me to compete at an international level. During my career, I never had any problems practicing in England, Canada, and the United States. My medical training in India gave me extraordinary clinical skills that my colleagues and patients recognized and lauded. I am grateful.

CHAPTER 16

Bina

Marriage is a turning point in everyone's life and it certainly was in mine. I had finished my internship at Trivandrum Medical College and like many medical students throughout India, I dreamed of advanced training in the West. I appreciated the rigorous education I received in India, but cutting-edge advances drew me to graduate programs in England and North America. In the late 60's and early 70's, a wave of Indian doctors immigrated to the United States, where they now constitute about 27 percent of the healthcare industry, and I wanted to join them. I passed the exams of the Educational Commission for Foreign Graduates, and started applying for residency programs in the United States.

Meanwhile, Bina's father and my own attended a wedding. In casual conversation my father proudly said that his son was going to America soon. In India it is customary to marry before you go for higher studies abroad, to provide stability and dispel the loneliness of bachelorhood in a strange land. It is the traditional wisdom of parents and we benefited from it. Bina's father said she had finished her master's degree and was waiting for further studies. My father told me about the chat and asked if I want to see Bina.

Along with both our parents, I met her at a cousin's house on February 13, 1975. Bina was 21, slim and beautiful with hair hanging below her waist. Her sweet nature and innocent smile, which occasionally widened into a broad grin, attracted me from the very first. The parents decided that we would make a good couple and our grandfathers, who were good friends, gave their blessings. It was an arranged marriage in all the traditional ways and my children still cannot get over the fact that we did not date or even really know each other before we wed.

About three months later, on May 29, 1975, we got married at Kottayam, Kerala. Bina had a beautiful hairdo with a touch of flowers and wore an embroidered white sari. A crowd of 1,500 attended. Many were Bina's parents' workers in the newspaper industry and the political friends of my new father-in-law, Dr. George Thomas, an ex-Member of the Legislative Assembly of Kerala. Others were friends of Mrs. Rachel Thomas, Bina's mother, a famous writer and speaker, and the chief editor of the popular Kerala weekly *Manorajayam*. There were also our friends from church, family, medical school, and her college.

Our marriage was founded on a platform of similar religion, education, and family background. The rest we had to build. Having grown up in a society with segregation of the sexes in classrooms, churches, and all public places, I was unskilled in the typical niceties men use to attract women, like flowers, clothes, jewelry, and compliments. But my common sense of respect and care for her proved enough to ignite her affection and our marriage blossomed into the family we built up.

Growing up in a family with a prominent politician as a father and a publisher and a literature scholar as her mother, Bina enriched my life. She was well read and her sharp intellect was obvious to anyone who spoke to her. She always kept her mind alert and informed. I worked long hours at the hospital and when I came home I often saw books and magazines on her bedside. She never missed an issue of *Newsweek* and *Time*, ever since her father started subscribing to them. As a publisher, her father had many other periodicals and she followed worldwide current affairs. I rarely opened books other than medical ones. Even now, whenever I come across a difficult word or usage, I consult her rather than a dictionary, and she answers graciously without making me feel inadequate. She brought vocabulary and general knowledge into my life.

Her affection for other people was clear even at the early stage of our marriage. My nieces and nephews were my cheerleaders before my marriage and when Bina came to my life they all said they were no match for the love Bina had in store for me. She was polite and respectful to all my family members and my mother adored her personality.

In fact, my mother loved her so much I took her with us on our honeymoon! It is still a family joke but it was a good time for me to get to know my bride, who was a stranger at that time. Come to think of it, it was not much of a honeymoon, but rather a day trip to a beautiful beach resort in Kovalam. We had our honeymoon later in life, when we had the means and time.

Soon after marriage I enrolled in the prestigious Christian Medical College at Vellore for my senior house-surgeoncy, and we stayed in a single room in the men's hostel. That is where we became partners and started building our dreams and future. Bina became a teacher at Ida Scudder School and the children and other teachers adored her. She joined the choir at the chapel to express her love for music. She brought melody into my life.

And celebrations! In my family there were no celebrations for birthdays or Christmas, but after Bina arrived she had cakes and candles and gifts for me during the first year of my marriage. Since then we have never missed any celebrations.

Watching her and living with her, I realized the value of human relationships on a different plane. She is generous with her compliments and overwhelms everyone with her unconditional love. She is very thoughtful and takes time for others and does just the right things in times of happiness and sorrow. Our family knows that I have increased my circle of friends because of her and so she brought camaraderie into my life.

I had six white shirts and a couple of pants in my medical school years. I never thought much about the way I dressed, other than following normal customs. Bina started paying attention to my shirts and ties and eventually I could not remember the last time I had bought my own ties, and so she brought fashion into my life.

She fully supported me in my career ambitions. I knew she loved me for who I was and I did not have much to pretend or hide from her to win her confidence early in life. This fact raised my trust and let me fully focus on my career, leaving the rest for her to manage. Her remarkable ability to adapt to any environment helped us in our life journey across the continents. Bina's emotional stability and maturity complimented my side of the equation. She was calm and poised and had visions for our future, and so she brought more security and aspiration into my life.

When our children went to school, Bina resumed her career as a teacher. She was hard-working and her superiors noticed that she was efficient and did her job without much fuss. These qualities got her promoted to the administrative level.

I still remember the smile I saw 33 years ago when I met her for the first time, a smile of hope, fear, doubt, and uncertainty. I saw the same smile when she looked at me after the marriage ceremony, when she must have been wondering what she was getting into, since we didn't know each other but would be partners for the rest of our lives. I know she must have thought, "What did I sign up for? What is in store for me living with this man I know only through my parents' description? What can we achieve in this world? Where will life take us?"

Slowly but steadily, the smile turned into a confident one when I went for a year of further training at Christian Medical College. She had a smile of exhilaration when we visited Buckingham Palace, the Tower of London, Hyde Park, Madame Tussaud's, the Lake District, and Edinburgh Castle. She had an eager smile when we crossed the White Cliffs of Dover to visit Europe. She had a happy smile when we went up the Eiffel Tower in Paris, rode the cable car on the Jungfrau in the Swiss Alps, gazed out at Lake Interlaken in Switzerland, and drove along the shores of the Rhine in Germany and up to St. Bernard Pass leading to Italy. She had a relaxed smile when we went past the geysers of Yellowstone Park, through the beautiful Tetons near Jackson Hole, and down to Los Angeles. She had a pleased smile when I established my medical practice in Los Angeles and traveled across the United States and the world, even snorkeling at the Great Barrier Reef in Australia. She would have that smile for 33 years, standing by me on every occasion, raising two children, and managing a teaching career.

Chapter 17

"You Should Live in California"

After I finished my year at Christian Medical College in Vellore, I was selected for post-graduate training in internal medicine at the University of Kerala. I fervently hoped to move to the United States in 1978 after I completed this program.

But the coin flipped again. In 1976, the U.S. Congress passed two laws that curtailed the number of foreign medical graduates that could enter the country. I had to move to the United States by January 1977 or I couldn't get in at all. However, my father passed away in July 1976, and Bina was due to give birth in February 1977. As strongly as I felt the pull of the West, I could hardly leave my recently widowed mother and my pregnant wife. The window closed.

However, in 1979 I was able to pursue higher studies in England, and Bina and I departed for London in April 1979, leaving our two-year-old son Vivek with Bina's parents. My dream of practicing in the West had finally come true, and I relished working in hospitals near London and in Chester, honing my skills in different specialties. Bina's mother brought Vivek to us that December, and between 1979 and 1982 we traveled all over Europe. We had embarked on our lifetime adventure.

But my English was still not good enough, and I knew it from the very first day I started working in Britain. Every time I saw a patient I had to write a letter back to the physician who referred the person to me. Making the diagnosis and determining the treatment were easy, but the next step — dictating that letter — was a nightmare.

Luckily I had a secretary who knew my struggle and she assured me that they had hired me not for my command of language but for my diagnostic skills and bedside care of patients. She asked me to tell her my thoughts and she produced wonderful, polished reports. To this day, I marvel how those perfect letters emerged from my dictation. The salutation was perfect, the language clear, and instructions well-outlined. The letters also had a beautiful ending that let the referring physician know I enjoyed seeing the person and that suggested keeping me in mind with future patients.

I learned an important life lesson from that experience: Circumstances and handicaps should not excuse us from achieving whatever we are created for. Scripture teaches us, "My Grace is sufficient for you." We can easily think that certain tragic, traumatic events happen to us alone and such a perspective makes us feel wounded and apart. I experienced this feeling, but by observing other people's lives, I realized it was a universal phenomenon. We don't appreciate what we have, but we fret about what we lack and make ourselves miserable over it. When I saw my secretary writing a letter for me, I marveled at her command of English and her ease at the typewriter. Of course, she told me she was British and English was her mother tongue! She in turn was fascinated by my diagnostic skills and ability to quickly figure out the right treatment for a patient.

I have come to the conclusion that life is full of compensations. You may be poor but rich in love. You may be depressed because of your circumstances but still able to offer friendship and caring to other people. You may have education but lack wisdom. You may have wealth but lack generosity in your heart. You may be tall but unable reach out to people in need. You may be born into a rich family but have lost compassion for the poor. You may be healthy but forget the suffering of the ill. You may be happy all the time but not know the distress of a person in mourning. You may be the most successful person in your career but a failure at home. You may have many friends because of your status but very few loyal ones.

Everyone, in every sphere, has areas for improvement. Recognize what you have, do the best with it, and strive to improve where you're deficient.

In 1982, Tara was born, and in the same year I was offered a residency in internal medicine at the University of Saskatchewan in Canada. The next three years were exhilarating. I loved the challenge of working under pressure, especially in the ICU and CCU. I developed a special interest in cardiology. I passed the board exams and became a Fellow of the Royal College of Physicians in 1985, fulfilling a great career goal.

A medical group asked me to join their practice in the town of Prince Albert, near Saskatoon in northern Saskatchewan, an area of bitterly cold winters. After 16 years of medical training on three continents, I was now a full-fledged specialist. Bina became a special-education teacher and joined the Prince Albert public schools teaching students with learning disabilities. I believed we would raise our family and live out the rest of our lives in Prince Albert.

My professional duties took me away from home for many hours and Bina did everything in a well-organized way to bring up the children. One day when I came back from a long weekend call at the hospital, Bina said, "Tara is walking now." Another day Bina was driving and I was sitting in the back seat with Tara, so I started reading stories to her. In astonishment she said, "Mom, Dad can read!" Bina had spent so much time reading to the kids that they had no idea I had this ability too!

There I appeared on TV for my first and only time. The town held its Cardiac Awareness Week, which promoted wellness and taught the public healthy living and lifestyle modification. As I was a leading physician in town with a large caseload of cardiac patients, the local TV station interviewed me. I discussed the importance of quitting smoking, exercising regularly, eating healthy low-fat food, and watching your weight.

Newspapers have mentioned me twice, once after the train wreck and again after my keynote speech to the Cancer Society of Prince Albert. There I told the audience about the role of cancer-producing agents in our day-to-day lives, and outlined steps to lower risk of the disease. I also gave them hope that research was progressing rapidly. One interesting area, I noted, was antibody-tagged chemotherapy or radiation therapy that attacked only cancer cells, minimizing the damage to the normal cells in the body. Cancer therapy in the future, I said, would use a kind of "smart bomb," targeting cancer cells like a heat-seeking missile, and the outlook for patients seemed very promising. The newspaper headline read: "Cancer Therapy Like War!" At that time, I had no idea that 16 years later I would be receiving the most advanced target-oriented chemotherapy myself.

Over the years, the chill of the Prince Albert winters started getting to us. I recalled an incident back in medical school. I lived in a mostly Hindu state and it was hard to find a Christian place of worship. Moreover, I had focused my mind intensely on keeping up with the high-pressure medical curriculum ahead of me. One day a missionary from Canada knocked at our door. He introduced himself as Mr. Erickson and he said he had heard that Christian students from Kerala were living in this building. He described his ministry and invited us to join him at his house on Sundays for breaking of bread and prayer time.

He lived in a spacious home with his wife and they used one of the rooms for prayer and Bible studies. About ten people gathered there on Sundays and he had Bible studies on Wednesdays as well. My cousin Gee-kutty and I enjoyed the fellowship for many years with him. He visited our homes in Kerala and we took him sightseeing all over the state so he could see the enchantment of the land and enjoy the tropical climate.

Once we were on a train journey in an open compartment and I saw him savoring the warm air through the window and gazing at the beautiful paddy fields and coconut groves. He leaned across the seat to me and said, "You should live in California." He said I would like the weather and assured me that I would feel at home in that new land.

I responded with an innocent smile. For a 19-year-old medical student who had no idea where this California was and didn't even know that I would be able to leave my country, it was just a passing notion. He whispered to me that he would pray for me, as many passengers in the compartment seemed curious to see a white missionary talking to a local lad. I added this wish to my prayer list from school days and just left it there.

But the frostiness of Canada made California seem very appealing. I never had a sweater in my life till I left Kerala, and now I owned many. One day in December 1988, I was perusing a medical journal when I came across an article by a name I recognized. Could it be my old friend Sethu? I saw a contact address at the end and I immediately wrote asking whether the author was the same Sethumadhavan who had attended medical school with me. A few days later the phone rang and we were in touch again.

Sethu invited me to visit him in Southern California, and in December 1989, I stepped off the plane in Los Angeles wearing five layers of clothes, including a heavy overcoat, lined boots, gloves and woolen hat. My friend looked at me and asked, "Why are you wearing all that in Southern California?" I told him that I had needed them when I'd boarded the plane from Saskatoon, where the temperature was -40 degrees.

He described the balminess of Southern California to me — it was 80 degrees that day in Los Angeles — and encouraged me to move closer to him and establish a practice. Even though I was happy in Prince Albert, the warmth and the challenge of working in a larger city and hospital beckoned. He helped me with all the contacts and visa formalities and finally in getting a medical license in California.

In March of 1990 I interviewed on the main campus of Kaiser Permanente Hospital at Panorama City, in Los Angeles. I had originally intended to go to a smaller, satellite clinic of this campus, but the medical director, looking at my credentials and hospital experience, recommended that I join the staff in the main one. The coin flipped again, and this became the hospital and campus I fell in love with.

One of the encouraging things I have learned in my life is that prayer is powerful and God answers prayer in many ways. God's timing may not be the same as ours, as God is eternal and time was given us to structure our lives. But the impossible dream of California had long fermented in my mind and been kept alive through prayer. It was fulfilled beyond my wildest dreams and I do indeed enjoy the warm California sunshine.

Even so, I felt a certain wariness about coming to the United States, mainly because of the negative stories you hear about legal issues in medicine. I also experienced the normal anxiety about starting a new practice in a new country at the age of 40 with two school-age children. A friend in Canada teased me, saying that I would be swapping my five layers of winter clothing for a bulletproof vest because of the crime rate in Los Angeles. The traffic congestion was another challenge when moving from a small town to a big city practice.

We shipped most of our belongings — furniture, utensils, beddings, and the rest — by a Mayflower van. But we couldn't ship our car and the moving van would take 10 days to reach Los Angeles. So we decided to make a holiday of it and drive from Prince Albert to Los Angeles, knowing the trip would be memorable for the children also.

We traveled through Montana, where the terrain changed from the flat Canadian plains we were used to. Further south, we had a fascinating stay in Yellowstone Park, where we saw waterfalls, bison, and Old Faithful. We lingered in Jackson Hole, in the beautiful Grand Tetons. Our son Vivek took a canoe trip down the Snake River and we drove alongside it stopping at viewpoints to watch him. Further south, we stayed in Las Vegas and found the magic of that neon city very intense.

After 10 days we reached Southern California and Sethu's home. His wife Geetha had arranged a place for us to stay and found schools for the children, and Bina had already set up an interview at a school for students with learning disabilities.

I started my practice at the Panorama City campus in the first week of July 1990. As an internist I loved it, as it had a nine-story hospital building, a busy and fully functional emergency room, and all the subspecialties except neurosurgery and cardiovascular surgery, right on the campus.

I found the transition very easy as I knew I had excellent training. With a bit of arrogance I can say that I knew my subject better than many around me, due to my extensive medical experience in three different countries.

However, it took me six months to get used to the traffic in Los Angeles. We managed to break into the local real estate market and bought our home, though houses in Los Angeles were three times as expensive as in Prince Albert. The children adapted well and Bina began her new job at school.

Within one week of starting at Panorama City, I had a patient with pneumonia. It was a complicated case so I asked for a consultation with a pulmonary specialist. Dr. Mathew, a physician in his 50s with a ponytail, who came to see my patient. Then he entered my office, discussed the treatment line with me in detail, and also talked to the family, as I was busy in my clinic. I saw that he had an excellent bedside manner, good communication skills, and overall an excellent attitude toward life and work. Once a year our departments in Southern California gathered for a symposium and at that time they honored one outstanding physician from each campus as the Internist of the Year. When I heard Dr. Mathew's name called out as the winner, I cheered as I was impressed with his work ethic and his reassuring manner with patients. In 2000, when I received the same award, it was gratifying to realize that colleagues recognize and reward professionalism and a dedicated attitude towards your vocation.

My career in Panorama City was very rewarding and I became more and more involved in departments, activities, and patient care programs. I was running the congestive heart failure clinic, hypertension clinic, and cholesterol clinic, as well as population care management, where we monitored all the preventive disease cases and recommendations and we carried out protocols for keeping a certain population — such as people with diabetes, hypertension, or cholesterol — under optimum care.

The Panorama campus was very friendly. I remember my nurse Sandy, who was a terrific, happy-go-lucky, cheerful person. She quickly learned my routine and was highly proactive in taking care of patients. Her communication skills were excellent, and patients loved her and cherished the time they spent with her and me during their visits. Lubia, our unit coordinator, was a tender, soft-spoken, cool-headed person who managed the staff in our module, took care of all patient complaints, and kept things running smoothly.

I had a large patient volume. Many Indian patients gravitated towards me, especially those who spoke Malayalam. A few Italian patients saw my last name, thought I was Italian, and came into my practice. I was sent a lot of difficult patients who needed to be managed. Many employees became my patients and also sent their family members for treatment. I think I put in my best effort and earned a good reputation on the campus. I received a lot of respect within the department and among my colleagues.

However, my friends in Canada had warned me that practicing in California was different from anywhere in the world. They were concerned about the high frequency of medical litigation. I reassured them that I had practiced medicine for more than 15 years and if I had never had a lawsuit in the early part of my career, when I was still learning, I had little chance of having one in my prime, with all my skill and experience.

But my friends' prediction came true one day when I opened my mail as usual and found a letter from an attorney notifying me of a lawsuit regarding a patient who had died of a heart attack in his fifties. After practicing medicine for so long with no complaints, the sight of this document was devastating. I went at once to Dr. Cohen, the assistant area medical director. My hands were shaking. My voice was stuttering. I told him about the legal action and the letter in my hand. What was I to do?

Since he was an experienced senior physician in an administrative position, I was relieved to see little panic on his face, but my heart raced as I desperately awaited his response. He reassured me that I was working in a part of the world where lawsuits were not unusual. They weren't personal, he said, and this one was probably aimed at the organization. He told me not to take it to heart but face it systematically and professionally, and he guided me to the legal department.

The head of the legal department was Dr. Paul, an ophthalmologist and a lawyer. I walked into his office and voiced my concern and fear. He too told me that practicing in this city you inevitably faced lawsuits. "You're like a circus performer here," he said. "You have to go out before the crowd all the time, but periodically you may fall and get injured. Don't let it keep you from enjoying the rewards of a medical practice."

Even though his words were reassuring I still could not process this event. I was humiliated. I felt that my very character was questioned and I was a failure in my profession. The emotional trauma and the internal dialogue disturbed me for a long time until the lawsuit had ended. Once you are in litigation you are not supposed to speak about it to your colleagues or anyone other than your attorney, so a loneliness builds up. But later I found out in talking to people that in fact almost everybody goes through this experience. You simply have to learn to deal with it as part of your career.

Chapter 18

Shift Beneath My Feet

On January 17, 1994, I reported for night call at 10 pm. During night call, you are in charge of all admissions to the medical floors and any emergencies in the hospital. You also handle all requests from the nursing staff with concerns about patients. You remain on duty till 8 am. Night call can be exhausting, and afterwards you generally feel like you've had jet lag for three days.

By 3 am things were slowing down, as they usually did, so I lay down in the call room and tried to catch some sleep. Around 4 am my bed and the whole room suddenly began jerking violently and I felt as if a 747 jumbo jet had landed in the parking lot. I jumped out of bed. The lights went off for an eyeblink, but then the hospital generator kicked in. I had never felt an earthquake before, but the rumbling and wild shaking made me think this might be the Big One everyone talked about.

I went outside and saw people standing in the parking lot and looking up at the hospital to see if it would fall. Since it was my first quake, I was confused and anxious, but I was also listening to other people's conversation to see how they planned to respond.

I went back into the building to see how the nursing staff and other people were doing. I was told there would be aftershocks and within a short time one actually struck. With panicked faces, people scrambled for shelter so the building wouldn't crush them if it collapsed. They found desks and benches to scrunch under every time an aftershock hit.

Since it was 4 am, I wasn't sure whether I should call home, and I wasn't even sure I could, since I heard that the phone lines were down. I was also uncertain that anyone at home 20 miles away would have felt the earthquake. Later I learned that the ground trembled very noticeably even in Las Vegas, 300 miles away.

I began pacing between the emergency room and the urgent care area in case any patients were seeking help. Slowly and steadily people started arriving in the emergency room with cuts and bruises from broken glass. I usually attend to medical patients, but on that day I had to do suturing and help put casts on the injured. Patients on respirators and feeding tubes who depended on electric power also came to the hospital because of the power outage at their homes.

By early morning extra staff members were arriving in the emergency area to help with the now-ceaseless flow of patients who needed care for the minor traumas they had suffered. I tried to call my home from hospital but all phone lines were dead. We had an understanding that if there was an emergency, we would call out of state to Bina's Aunt Leela. So I tried the long distance number and reached her. She said that, yes, she heard from Bina that there was an earthquake and everybody was safe.

By 9 o'clock enough staff had arrived on site, so I finished my work and drove home. The streets were very quiet and no traffic lights were working, so I had to stop at every intersection and check for oncoming traffic.

When I finally reached home, Bina and the children were busy cleaning up the mess. Bina said that she had woken up at 4 am in pitch darkness to a thunderous sound as if a freight train were roaring through the house. She was confused that I was not getting up, because in her shock she had forgotten that I was at the hospital. As soon as the shaking stopped, she and the children ran outside.

Once back inside, she saw that the entire contents of the refrigerator had tumbled out onto the floor and the television had fallen down. The china cabinet had shifted and leaned against the wall. The bookshelves were completely empty and there was no water or gas. My son took the trashcan and skateboard out to the swimming pool and brought water into the house to use in the toilet and for washing.

The whole neighborhood came together and people who owned barbecues started making coffee and shared their bread and milk. For the rest of the day we listened to news of damage around Los Angeles on the radio. We found out that the fault line ran directly under our area, which became famous because the temblor was called the Northridge Quake. Our cousin Sunny and friends Nicky and Andy came and fixed all the blinds, cleaned up all the broken glass, and tried to put the house back in order.

I was uneasy for the next few night calls because I couldn't help reliving the sounds and feelings of this unforgettable event. But soon I was enjoying my interactions with my patients again and, as always, I found contact with each of them educational as well as fulfilling. I was fully contented and happy with my career until late 2003, when the coin flipped again.

Parents M.P. Varughese and Thankamma Varughese

A rare family picture. Top row (left to right): Joseph, father M.P. Varughese, brother George, brother Philip, maternal grandfather P.I. Joseph, brother-in-law Thomas Mathew, niece Valsamma. Sitting (left to right): Paternal grandmother, mother Thankamma, aunt Mariamma, sister Daisykochamma, nephew Prasad, maternal grandmother, sister Lillykochamma. Front row (left to right): sister Molly, niece Annie, nephew Suku, niece Leelamma

Maternal grandparents' home in Punnavely

Wedding Day: Joseph and Bina. May 29th, 1975

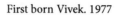
First born Vivek. 1977

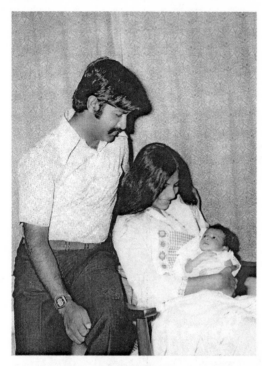

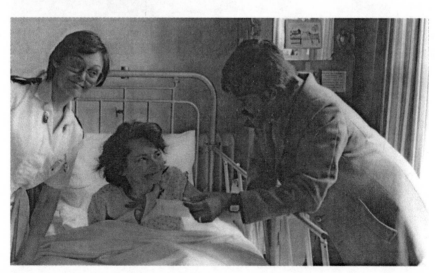
Young house surgeon in Chester, England. 1979

Final year residents –University of Saskatchewan, Canada. Joseph– middle row, second from left

Start of a life-long fascination with computers and technology

Beloved sister–Lillykochamma

The siblings gather together to see if they are potential donors.
Left to right: Philip, Joseph, George, Molly

Sethu and Joseph–young medical
students 1973

Sethu and Joseph–35 years later

Trip to India 2006

PART II

TAILS

CHAPTER 19

Lumps

On December 3, 2003, I parked the car in the usual place at the hospital. I usually rushed through the parking lot adjusting my white coat and stethoscope. On that day, I wore a short-sleeved blue shirt and black pants. My pager and cell phone were at home. My wife held my hand and I walked with hesitant strides, avoiding eye contact with the employees and co-workers. The corridor where I normally paced up and down so confidently now seemed like a strange path to an unknown destination. I tucked my right hand in my pocket instead of waving it to familiar patients and colleagues.

My gaze locked on the sign hanging near the receptionist: "Hematology Oncology Patient Waiting Area." Even though I had seen it a thousand times, my heart missed a beat this time. Then the receptionist placed an ID bracelet with my name and medical record number on my right hand.

I sat in the waiting room, feeling suffocated. I gazed around at the other patients. Two were reading, while others sat there with eyes closed. Running my hand over my thick hair, I noticed a few patients with bald scalps. I realized that soon I might look like them. I tried to control my tears but could not.

The nurse opened the door to the waiting room and called, "Dr. Var-ughese!" I saw all the patients looking at us with an unspoken question in their eyes: "Why is the doctor sitting in the patients' waiting room?"

I had had low back pain for a few weeks. The past weekend while do-ing my rounds, I went down to the emergency room and chatted with the physicians, and they suggested a CT scan of my abdomen. I did the CT scan and continued my rounds.

When I returned to the ER I saw a little conference between the radiolo-gist and the emergency physician. I was hoping that I had a normal scan, but they told me that I had 15 enlarged nodes in my abdomen. Those nodes could be tumors.

On that day in December I had come to see my colleague Dr. Nathan, an oncologist, to learn if I really had cancer or another condition, like sarcoidosis or tuberculosis. He entered with a poker face. I wondered what was wrong with him. I thought to myself,"I am your friend. Why are you so serious? Tell me that it is tuberculosis, as I might have been exposed to it in India, and send me next door to the infectious disease specialist. Or call it sarcoidosis and give me some steroids."

But he said he had reviewed my CT scan and wanted to investigate it further. He said I would need a CT-guided biopsy of one of the enlarged lymph nodes and they would keep me in the hospital for a PET scan and other tests.

In a daze, I heard my wife asking some questions. Then they took me to the infusion room to get an IV line and prepare for the biopsy. I looked at my elbow and forearms. I didn't have many visible veins, so how in the world were they going to get intravenous access? The nurse seemed to be confident and got an IV line without much trouble, remarking, "This vein is even good for chemo infusion."

My mind started to deny it. I told myself that I didn't need chemo-therapy, that I was only here for the test and I would simply get steroids or anti-tuberculosis medicine and go home.

I had admitted countless patients to the 6th floor, and now, after the bi-opsy, they took me to Room 620 on that same floor. A movie started playing in my head of all the patients I had seen in that room. Many were very ill, a few had died, and I clearly saw their faces in my mind. My thoughts began racing unstoppably, only to be distracted by my wife, daughter, and son, who were at my bedside.

Over the next four days I went through a whirlwind of tests, including a PET scan, bone scan, and colonoscopy. They wheeled me in and out of the room for tests on a gurney, and I covered my face so no one could identify me. I didn't want anybody to see that I was a patient now. I was in total denial. But the nursing staff was extra careful to see that I was comfortable. They blocked out my name on the board for privacy reasons and deflected the questions of employees who wondered why I was in this room.

The fine needle biopsy results came back as "large B cell non-Hodgkin's lymphoma."

Images of patients I had lost to similar conditions flashed over my mind's screen. I remembered a 36-year-old businessman dying of leukemia and his wife and two children sitting at his bedside. I remembered the 64-year-old man who died of myeloma and suffered extreme pain near the end. I remembered the sobbing teenaged girl whose father was dying from uncontrollable bleeding due to cancer. I remembered the shrill cry of a young lady with severe bone pain trying to find a comfortable position. I remembered the Filipina lady in her sixties coming to me with massive bloating of her face due to obstruction of veins in her chest. I remembered the diabetic black lady who had terminal cancer and huge abdominal swelling from accumulating fluid, advising me to buy my first home in Los Angeles as soon as I moved here (wonderful advice). I remembered the face of a 21-year-old cousin in India who said good-bye to us to go to the hospital for treatment but never returned.

Like a broken record, the images played in my head and I wondered where destiny had charted my course. How had this happened to me? Why had it hit me now, when I was only 53, at the peak of my career, with everything going well for me? I had prayed to God and gone to church. I had given every other human greater respect than myself. Why at this time, when I was a much-appreciated and even honored physician on the campus, did I have to sit still and watch this movie in my mind?

I had come to the West with a suitcase full of books, the basic essentials, and $30 in my pocket. Now I had everything I wanted. I was contributing significantly to society, paying my taxes on time, and providing care for many patients. Why, out of 250 doctors at this hospital, had cancer hit me? Why did I, who led a disciplined life with no cancer-producing risk, become the victim? I really felt victimized. I felt afraid, I felt deflated, I felt lonely. I felt slammed by a huge invisible force. I knew there was a lot to endure before I could even think of getting back to work.

Yes, getting back to work was my goal. Maybe it's because I am an immigrant here, but I always enjoyed my work in whatever environment I found myself. I never complained, even when the circumstances were bad or there were others to blame. I have lived a life of gratitude because I think I have more than I deserve. I have given my best to my patients and colleagues. I enjoyed everything new and every challenge and change I faced in my life. Having crossed three oceans and worked in four different countries, I developed a vast spectrum of experience and I used it to help my patients. I knew my patients and co-workers liked me. I felt I was making significant contributions to the institution.

Now I lay in a hospital bed with intravenous fluid running through my body and my mind pondering questions: What does the scientific data say? How will my body react to chemotherapy? Since I had no prominent veins in my arms, how would they get all the blood needed to monitor my treatment and how would they infuse all these toxic medicines into my system? What was in store for me?

I used to get a little annoyed when a patient asked for a referral for a second opinion. My internal dialogue would go into action and say, "Don't you trust me? I have 16 years of medical training. I have practiced medicine in many different countries. I have passed all the medical board examinations. My credentials are impeccable and you want me to send you for a second opinion?!" Aloud, I'd say, perhaps unenthusiastically, "Okay, I will."

But now, when I myself faced the diagnosis of cancer, I wanted a second opinion at once, mainly because I was in total denial and I wanted to make sure that I had the right diagnosis and treatment options. Help came from one of my friends, Dr. Fred Rosenfelt, a renowned oncologist and lymphoma specialist. Fred's wife Nancy is the director of Bina's school, Summit View. We used to accompany them to conferences related to their work, had visited many places and became close over time. So now, from my hospital room, I did not hesitate to ask Fred to review my case and the biopsy slides to give his opinion. Fred is a soft-spoken person with a highly regarded oncology practice in Los Angeles. He has excellent connections and he is also affiliated with prestigious teaching hospitals. He told me to send all the slides to him. After reviewing them with the pathologist, he confirmed the diagnosis.

Dr. Ashok Reddy, chief of surgery in our institution and a family friend, came to my bedside. He is a gentle man with magic surgical hands. Without much conversation but with reassuring eyes, he examined my neck and said, "I will put a Port-a-Cath on your right side." A Port-a-Cath is a catheter inserted into your chest to administer chemotherapy. The next day I was wheeled to the OR. My neighbor Ophelia, an anesthetist nurse practitioner, helped me through anesthesia with much concern in her eyes.

I was discharged on a Friday after completing all the tests, still awaiting the results of a few. The plant manager of our institution, Rick Wyke, showed up in my room and volunteered to push my wheelchair to the car in the parking lot.

That weekend was very eventful because there were so many phone calls from all over the world asking about my condition and the plans for my treatment, as well as visits from nearby friends and family.

CHAPTER 20

WBC: 3.2

D r. Nathan, my oncologist, took full charge. He has been a friend and colleague for many years. We used to have lunch together, used to sit and laugh and talk about our families, world affairs, and department politics. Now suddenly he became my lifeline. His calm nature and unwavering determination to carry me through the disease gave me more assurance. And he was unambiguous about the next step to take: chemotherapy.

I have been reading the Bible since childhood. It is the one book I have read throughout my life, wherever I have been. I rarely missed my daily prayers and I thought I had a good relationship with God, but now I faced the prime decision on the most important condition in my life. Did I have the faith to ask God for complete healing? Did I fully trust the medical field or should I forsake it and rely on sheer faith?

My oldest sister Lillykochamma from India called and said she was going to pray as my mother had while I was in medical school. My older brother George from Muscat called and said God was in control. Our parents had led a good life. We had all led principled lives. So God would hear our prayers and provide healing for us. My brother Philip from India called and said God's thoughts were not like man's thoughts, so healing was on the way and I should have faith. My younger sister Molly from

Michigan called and said, "Be strong in your belief and God will answer your prayers."

While my spiritual mind wanted to adhere to the faith of my forefathers, my logical mind analyzed everything and decided that I had to go through the chemotherapy.

Yet I wondered where I would get the fortitude to endure this treatment. Then I realized that a band of colleagues, cardiologists, nuclear medicine specialists, gastroenterologists, and internists had all assembled behind Dr. Nathan. I felt embraced by the brotherhood and sisterhood of colleagues and friends, and along with my family they were a tower of strength for me at this time. I realized that family, faith, and friends were the three key ingredients, along with excellent medical care, to see me through the ordeal ahead.

The treatment planned was Rituxan: CHOP chemotherapy. (CHOP stands for: cyclophosphamide, hydroxydaunorubicin, Oncovin, and prednisone/prednisolone.) I would undergo six cycles at three-week intervals. I was fully confident that after the last one I could return to my work, since remission seemed the most likely outcome from my reading of the literature and statistics. I braced myself to endure whatever inconveniences I might encounter at this stage.

Chemotherapy was to start Monday morning, and the weekend before was probably the longest ever for our family. My friend and surgeon, Dr. Ashok Reddy, assured the children that lymphoma was a curable cancer and that's all they wanted to hear. Bina's aunt Glennie had developed lymphoma at 45 and was still healthy and traveling the world at 72. So Bina anchored onto that and tried to steel herself for the chemotherapy that I faced.

To me, none of these helped. My mind started analyzing everything. My mind began re-reviewing the patients I had seen. My mind wanted to examine all the medical literature. My mind wanted to see all the side effects I would face. I anticipated all the complications and worst-case scenarios, and so the countdown to Monday morning was a dreadful time in my life.

That Saturday I had looked in the mirror and run my hands through my hair. I tried to comb it. It was very thick and I remembered the many times I had broken the comb because of its thickness. Since my teenage years I had always carried a comb in my pocket and I periodically smoothed my hair and reset it. I had received many compliments on it and, I should admit, I have been a little proud of it. My colleagues once teased me, after one stormy night call, asking how come my hairstyle had not changed.

Now I realized it was all going to disappear and I would be walking around bald. Since this was utterly predictable, my son took me to the barbershop the day after chemotherapy began and had my head shaved. To sympathize with me, he also shaved his head.

My wife had already consulted people about places that sold wigs, and she sensed my desperation. So she told me gently that we should visit a shop in Hollywood to customize a wig that would look exactly like my hair. I agreed and we got a wig. It gave me some confidence that once I lost my hair I could still meet other people without being self-conscious about it. The wig gave me a false sense of vanity and helped me go in for my chemotherapy and later get out and feel near normal, though I stayed home most days.

The next problem was my mustache. I had one since I was 15, and I always cared for it well. Friends had complimented me on it too, saying it added to my personality and distinctiveness. One day a few years ago, I shaved it off and my kids did not recognize me. They didn't even want to get in my car when I pulled in to pick them up from the school. The thought that I was going to lose my mustache was also very painful to me. In the big picture it may seem like vanity, but at that moment it appeared the biggest burden I had to bear. Of course I did lose my mustache. I also lost my eyebrows and eyelashes, which added to the agony of facing my new appearance.

My wife prepared the house for my chemotherapy. The refrigerators were cleaned up and loaded with food. Bina knew that I had to have fresh, and newly cooked food every day for the next few weeks, as long as I was undergoing chemotherapy. Bina's Aunt Leela from Seattle came down to be with us. She is a dietitian and Bina's lifeline. She took Bina to the grocery store to choose foods I might be able to take when the nausea and vomiting peaked.

Monday morning with a heavy heart, teary eyes, and hesitant steps, we went to the hematology-oncology clinic infusion center. Since I already had the Port-a-Cath, the nurse started the intravenous line and informed me about the side effects of all the medicines I was getting. Even before she withdrew the needle the first time, I started feeling sick to my stomach.

We drove home, and it did not take long before I needed a bedside bucket to take care of my nausea. Food started to smell unpleasant and soon I noticed it had no taste at all.

I have seen people with vomiting and have managed people with vomiting, but when it hit me, I realized it was worse than I'd thought. My whole gastrointestinal system turned upside down, to the point that I couldn't even swallow saliva. My oncologist had warned me not to get dehydrated, yet even taking a sip of water shook my whole system. Though I was taking high doses of anti-nausea medication, the nausea and vomiting were miserable. Moreover, with the total loss of taste sensation, the bowel functions completely change and become very unpredictable. Sleep gets disturbed due to pain, fatigue, and nausea.

Bina had stacked different types of juice on my bedside table so I could sip from different ones and keep some of them down. She started making khanji, rice soup, so that I got carbohydrates. She tried to make me drink high-calorie shakes, but I could not down them. Family and friends kept telling me to close my eyes and drink the shake. When taste and smell are gone, no amount of pressure helps, but they did what they felt best for my well-being. I knew that I needed plenty of nutrition, but my stomach did not get the message and I could not help succumbing to my stomach rather than my brain and the urgings of people around me.

Hoping that this too would pass, I braced myself and struggled through the treatment days. Chemotherapy requires constant monitoring with frequent blood tests, and one of the most important is the count of white cells, which protect our body from infection.

I went for my first blood test after the chemotherapy. I waited for the results and then I saw the printout in my hand: WBC (white blood count) 3.2. Normal is between 4.3 and 10.8, and I have seen abnormal values a thousand times. But when I saw my name on top and the number 3.2, the experience was totally different. A trembling, crushing sensation went through my heart. The white cells protect against infection, and a sense of vulnerability rushed in.

I quickly looked around to see if anyone was sneezing or coughing. I started covering my face with a handkerchief to keep germs out. A series of thoughts coursed through my mind. I was not able to brush my teeth vigorously and I had to avoid cutting or bruising my hand because anything could trigger an infection. I knew that germs were the biggest enemy during chemotherapy and I had to take extra precautions to keep them out.

The phone calls from the family and friends gave me enough distractions, but every day seemed darker than the last as the impact of chemotherapy mounted. Intellectually, I had foreseen all the side effects, but they were hard to deal with emotionally when they started happening one by one. Frankly, I could not believe the extent of them and the impact on my body and mind. I felt like the traveler who reads about the details of his destination, and then lands there, confronts its full dimensions, and finds a very, very different experience.

I was confined to bed most of the time, except for bathroom needs and eating. A warm electric blanket came handy and I was reluctant to leave that comfort zone. I tried to sleep as much as possible, keeping my eyes closed. I started losing interest in everything around me except for symptoms that popped up one by one.

Time had slowed down. It was strolling rather than running, yet it was the competitor I was racing against. Time seemed to be my enemy. The moments turned against me. The times I went to the bed and did not fall asleep, the times I woke up and could not go back to sleep, the times I tried to eat and couldn't, the times I made a drink and was unable to gulp it down. The times I wanted to look at flowers and my eyes started tearing; the times I wanted to read and the letters became a blur; the times

I wanted to watch TV and the picture grew fuzzy; the times I wanted to write and the paper got soaked with my tears. Fatigue set in, everything moved slowly, and the clock ticked by in seconds — but for me time was measured in number of times I vomited or felt miserable from the side effects of the therapy.

The miracle of normal life and my prestigious career had become a tragedy when cancer hit me and moved me to the other side of the stethoscope. And when I saw my white blood count going down, my fretfulness started going up. I felt an anxiety mixed with frustration and helplessness. I was wondering what the next step was.

With nervous eyes and no doubt a doomed face, I entered the office of Dr. Nathan, my oncologist and friend. I had the results of my blood tests in my hands. He made me sit down next to him and recommended the injection of Neupogen, which would temporarily raise the blood counts. I was a bit more at ease and went home with a prescription to take the injections at home myself. Even though I have written so many prescriptions and given so much advice to patients, I walked out of that office with a lesson: Every word a doctor speaks and every expression on a doctor's face has a lasting impact on the patient's mind.

I realized that day how much it means to empathize with a patient, to be fully aware of the extent of the person's anxiety and how much reassurance he or she needs. Moreover, the hope that the doctor can help you in any situation is very important.

And Dr. Nathan was right. My count went up with the Neupogen injections and I felt very relieved and happy.

CHAPTER 21

Becoming a Patient

What is it like to be a patient? The question came home to me during my treatment. I had been a physician for 30 years and I had come across many types of patients. So did I know what it was like to actually be a patient?

Of course I did, I thought. I looked after patients all the time. Every day I saw them, greeted them, called them, examined them, and took care of their needs. I have seen my patients cry when they learned they had a serious illness. I have seen them get frustrated when I asked them to go through certain procedures and occasionally I have seen them grow angry when things didn't turn out well.

So I knew how to approach being a patient. I had to be in the good graces of my physician, establish a strong rapport with him or her, and express my concerns, and he or she in turn would take care of my physical and mental needs. Would it be a big deal to accept the role? I didn't think so, as I had been a patient after the train wreck in India and I had had knee surgery as well as the usual colds and coughs.

But it all looked different when I faced a life-threatening illness. The biggest challenge was surrendering my individuality as a doctor. And I had to deal with issues arising from the fact that I was a patient in my own institution. The corridors I had strolled confidently now changed to ones where I walked with my head down and stood in line for blood tests and procedures. The lab technicians and others I used to give orders to in my white coat now occasionally needed a reminder that I had worked there. The receptionist who asked for my second ID needed a prompt before she seemed to realize that I had been a physician at this place. The co-workers who used to greet me and ask about the day's events now inquired sympathetically about my general health. The pharmacist asked why I was taking all these medications and what had happened. Occasionally I got a curious question from a co-worker about whether I was coming back to work, ever. The security guard at the gate would take a second glance at me, looking for my white coat or the ID card on my shirt. Now and then a patient of mine spotted me in the labs and asked what I was doing there. The whole interpersonal dynamic on the campus had changed. And the questions from family members and friends about why this illness had struck me at this time added to the insecurity growing inside me.

I found it difficult to give up my controlling personality as a physician and become a normal patient. Initially, I struggled with the idea that I deserved more than other people because I worked there. For instance, I often grew restless waiting my turn to see the provider. I have had patients get upset at me for making them sit there in the waiting room and I used to joke that it was called the "waiting room," not the "recreation room," so they had to wait to see me. As a patient myself, I understood their frustration better.

I also had to accept guilt feelings about being a patient. The taboo linked to cancer and severe illness moved my deeper consciousness and started flinging strange questions at me. The comments from friends and family about why I had developed such a disease at this stage of my life were weakening me. There were even suggestions that I had gotten cancer because of my lack of faith in God, the processed food I ate, and the environment I chose to live in. My mind started asking what I had done wrong. I never smoked and never ate or drank too much. I followed my exercise program and led a clean life in the eyes of the society and family. Like every other patient I know, I started asking how and why.

The biggest problem was my identity crisis. I had been a physician all my life. I spent all my formative years thinking about becoming a doctor and throughout my training I focused like a laser beam on getting the maximum out of it. As a physician I spent all my energy taking care of patients. I treasured my career.

Suddenly I noticed my pager was not going off, my phone was not ringing as before, and nobody was knocking at my door for my opinion. All I heard were sympathetic questions about my state of health, and gradually I learned to accept my new role and cope with it.

Yet it etched a deep wound in my personality. In a short time I lost my career, my earning capacity, my appearance, my ego, my confidence, my strength, my stamina, and my rational mind. I felt like a captain trying to patch leaks in a sinking ship. Like the captain I sent out SOS signals to my physicians to get me the best treatment, to my relatives to support me in prayer, to my friends to cheer me up, and to my family to see me through this crisis.

My wife Bina was the one who got the essence of my desperate message. She rose to the occasion and started taking charge of things. She had to worry about my ongoing care during chemotherapy, watch my diet, and arrange for me to have rest during the day, all in a very methodical manner. She had to handle all communications with family and physicians. To drive me to and from the hospital for tests, watch for the results, and take measures in response to them. To help me with daily activities. To shield me from visitors with colds and coughs and to provide meticulous hygiene in general. To reassure the children that I would get better soon. To manage the finances of the house, paying bills and handling the expenses that revolved around my illness. To juggle it all with her responsibilities as an administrator at a school.

She carried out all these tasks with good-spirited optimism in spite of my gloomy outlook. She listened to my complaints and vigilantly examined my symptoms to make sure she was attending to all of them effectively. She had to help invigorate my inner health, as I was losing my zest for life. She knew that I could easily fall into depression, as she had seen it happen after the death of my mother and during a short period in England. (In fact, I had concealed trauma which would later surface as depression and anxiety.) She had to sort out all the advice coming at us from all sides about what to eat and not eat, when to sleep, what to read, where to go, what to avoid.

My faith must have helped me be a patient. I have had a good prayer life. I used to pray daily for the wisdom and ability to do my work well. Even though these were self-centered prayers for me to excel, they were pleasurable and rewarding.

But when I became a patient, the intensity of the prayer and the urgency of my request reached a different scale. I prayed every day with tears running down my cheeks. I prayed like a wounded animal seeking escape from a predator. I prayed as if I wanted the full healing power of God beamed down on me at my command. I sent out messages to all those who could to pray for my recovery.

I had never prayed like this in my life and looking back now I can see that prayer is a wonderful tool. It readies your mind to make the right decisions. It prepares you for your treatment and it plays an especially big role in helping you accept your vulnerability as a patient and your dependence on God's provision. Even though doubts crept in many times and shook my faith, I had something to hang onto.

As a physician I had advantages and disadvantages. Among the advantages, I had access to the best medical personnel and I could discuss the options with them very openly. But there was a tremendous drawback to understanding the many side effects, the prognosis, and the destinations my symptoms could lead me to. This knowledge made me miserable and my emotions were totally unmanageable.

I started analyzing every little symptom, and every prescribed medication needed my analytical mind's approval. I had to process all the possible side effects of the chemical to be infused. Common symptoms often made me jump to unsound conclusions. If I got a chest pain, I thought I was heading for a heart attack. If I got a headache, I thought I might have meningitis. If I got a stomach cramp, I conjured up appendicitis. If I coughed twice, I felt I had pneumonia. I dwelt on the worst-case scenarios for all possible side effects and complications of the chemotherapy medications during recovery.

My mind was constantly watchful, to the point that I often felt paralyzed. Many days I felt total numbness in my body except for the tears running down my cheeks. At times I wished I was ignorant of my plight and had higher hopes of healing, rather than wasting my energy in worry about all the possible complications.

I have discussed this situation with my physician colleagues and they have validated it, as they know how our minds work once we understand the disease process. I have heard the adage "ignorance is bliss," and in my case I wish it applied. I suffered rather more than the average patient.

Chapter 22

Verdict

At home I gazed out my bedroom window for hours, watching the thick bush with its red berries and the squirrels playing on the branches. The mountain beyond our backyard was very serene and comforting. The community where I lived had only 70 houses and the streets were very quiet.

Apart from the physical discomfort, everything else was conducive to proper rest and recuperation. The towels in bathrooms were changed every day. Drinking water had been set aside and palatable beverages to sip lay on the bedside table. I had an iPod with meditation music and healing songs. My family bought a plasma TV and mounted it in my bedroom. They had taken charge of everything and I simply had to deal with the nausea and fatigue.

When nothing else worked, I reached out for the sleeping pills my physician prescribed. Sleep is very important during chemotherapy. It helps you to pass the slog time. It helps your body restore itself. It helps you forget some of the distress during the treatment. I used to sleep many times during the day. Yet though there was little pain at first, being more and more bedbound started to take a toll on my mind and body.

The support from my family helped me most. Cancer is a destructive disease, but it did not destroy our family bond. In fact, it brought us closer.

During my career my wife had mainly taken care of my children. I was involved as much as my busy schedule allowed. I have not heard complaints from my children that I didn't spend time with them. In fact, Tara can sit down with anyone and show all kinds of videos of our precious family time.

Once I became sick, I saw swift role reversals. Vivek, who had not been keen on sitting down with me for conversation, was suddenly at my bedside asking questions and letting me talk to him. He spent far more time with me than ever before. He also took over all the mundane tasks of running the home that I had done. He kept the garage in order, the sprinklers regulated, and the garbage disposed of on time. He stocked the refrigerator in the garage with drinks I liked. He became very aware of my bodily weaknesses and assisted me whenever I needed help. Driving to and from the clinics was an added chore for my children.

Tara was always a daddy's girl but the disease made her cling to me more and become attentive to all my comforts. I needed hot water bottles, tea whenever my mouth got dry, and snacks. She would find my misplaced reading glasses and return them to their original position. She was a big help to her mother in household chores like doing the laundry, helping buy groceries for her mom to cook, and of course constantly being my cheerleader so that I wouldn't sink into sadness. She brought out her childhood stories to keep me amused. She played videos of our family outings in Canada and, later, our vacation in India. She related how I had taken her skiing in Canada and roller-skating in the indoor arena. She used to come home from school with ice-cold hands, as she would lose her mittens, and she told me how I had kept her hands under warm running water to stop the pain from the bitter chill.

Bina's challenge was many-sided. She had to multitask her demanding job as a school curriculum coordinator with her new roles as caretaker for a sick husband with a devastating illness, and keeper of the financial engine to keep the household running. She executed the paperwork for long-term sick leave, disability payments, and social security benefits, and she needed extra time in the day to communicate to friends nearby and all the relatives around the world. The normal family dynamic had changed and she had to find new ways to orchestrate running a house and look after a sick husband.

Indeed, she became my life-line. My emotions were at their lowest and she helped me elevate them enough to get through the rigorous treatment. Physically, I became weak and needed more and more help. She had to sacrifice her own sleep to attend to my needs but also had to keep a job at school, carry out all the projects there, and meet the deadlines. She vigilantly watched over medical complications and communicated very well with the attending physicians. She meticulously kept track of all medications and attended to my complete nutritional needs. Only God can reward her for the care and devotion she has poured into our family.

My friends used to say Bina was like the wife described in Proverbs 31, with all the fine virtues a spouse needs, and they proved invaluable for our family when a crisis hit us. My friends observed her unwavering determination to see me through and they stepped in to support us.

There is a saying that friends are flowers in the garden of life. Luckily we are blessed with good ones. As soon as the diagnosis was announced, they arrived with their full ammunition of friendship. Dr. Sethu Madhavan was devastated by the news. He and his wife Geetha at once reached out, sharing in our concerns and helping us in many ways like bringing home-cooked meals and taking us out to dinner. Dr. Ashok Reddy and his wife Saranya were very sympathetic and attentive to our emotional state, reassuring the children about the prognosis of lymphoma and accompanying us all throughout the stages of treatment, from the first preparatory procedures for chemotherapy. My cousin Sunny and his wife Kunjumol, their son Vinoj and his wife Jenni were towers of strength. My neighbor Andy is an outdoorsman and a marathon runner. He is not very good with emotions and sympathy, yet he patiently made me go from baby steps to long walks during my chemotherapy and recuperation. He was there for our kids any time, a phone call away. Dr. Iyengar and Keerthi were friends from Canada. They visited us often, brought us food, and constantly reassured us that they were alongside us on this journey. Bina's childhood friend Nalini and her husband Nicky comforted and supported us. All of them were there to calm our fears and share our hopes. Other friends watched us from the distance, not knowing what to say or do other than make occasional phone calls. Friends separate to different tiers during trials like this. Some get closer, some observe from farther away, and some don't know what to do.

My hope and prayers lay in the six cycles of chemotherapy, and after they ended it was time to check my CT and PET scans to discover my response to the treatment. Almost every tumor area had disappeared. However, the CT scan showed one area of lymph node enlargement and the same region lit up on the PET.

I struggled with my emotions once I learned that chemotherapy had not contained the disease. The six cycles were going to put me in remission and let me get back to my normal work, I had thought. I had followed the medical advances. I knew my illness was curable. But when I saw this residual cancer, I felt like the hunter who has left his guns in the truck, hiked across the grasslands, and suddenly come face to face with a hungry lion. My mind and body began disconnecting. Once again I started envisioning worst-case scenarios. I did not realize that when the body grows weak the mind can too.

My guilt also became worse, and a tremendous amount of it lay trapped somewhere in that emotional package. As before, my mind wandered and repeatedly asked: What should I have done? Where did I go wrong? What should I have avoided? I hardly had the answers to these questions, but my mind never stopped raising them. In addition, you hear insinuations from some of your relatives that maybe you should have led a purer life or walked closer to God. But all those suggestions meant little now, because I was already ill. No amount of looking back would help me now, so I had to process these comments in my own way, listening to them, dealing with them internally, and then trying to respond gently. There was definitely an outpouring of love, care, concern, and blessings, but they were not enough to quell the fear, suspicion, anxiety, and uncertainty, the picture of doom that was so vivid inside me. So my emotional struggle intensified despite the consolations from family and friends, and the assurance from Bina and the children that this was not my fault.

I have always been a reader of self-help books. My shelves abound with them, from my first copy of *How to Win Friends and Influence People* by Dale Carnegie to the ultimate self-help book, the Holy Bible. I took many ideas from motivational gurus and grappled with them. I have attended seminars by Anthony Robbins, read all his books, and even walked on a bed of hot coals for the ultimate mental conditioning. I have followed the principles in *Seven Habits of Highly Effective People*, by Steven Covey. I have listened to many tapes and CDs on how to best shape your life. I have taken classes in yoga and meditation. I have memorized scripture and can recite it when needed. I spent two years at an evening Bible college studying the holy book from Genesis to Revelation, and I have a sound knowledge of theology. Although my faith was strong and the assurance of eternal life after death was built firmly into my mind, doubts crept in.

Many friends and family told me that now was the time to take full command of my mind and fight this disease. But I did not process the advice well at the time. Fight the disease? Was this a battle? In any battle the stronger party wins. Who was I to "fight" against a malady like cancer and think I could win? Instead of remembering people that said, "I wrestled cancer and beat it.", my mind alerted me to all the cases where I had seen patients perish. Why should I be the exception? Was there much point in "fighting this disease"?

My childhood memories came back to me and they were not much help. Whenever I had fought fear or anxiety, I had lost. I had managed to avoid or escape them sometimes, but I was never victorious. Fear and insecurity are foes I have battled all my life and now I had another enemy to "fight"?

People also suggested I be "strong." Again, the word raised questions. How can you be strong when chemotherapy is weakening your body every day? When I tried to walk to the bathroom, my legs felt like noodles. When I tried to climb the stairs, they seemed like mountains and I had to use all the strength in my hands to steady myself and take them one at a time.

How could I be strong with this debilitation setting in? Unless you expect me to work miracles, I thought, please don't tell me that.

So I was in a very bad situation and the advice I received— be strong, fight this, eat this food, walk this far, sleep this much, exercise, read, play video games, watch funny movies, do this, do that — was not helping. I realize that they had to give me what they thought was the best advice, but in real life you simply couldn't apply it on command.

A deep sense of sorrow floats in your mind from the emotional trauma, the physical weakness, and that distinctive feeling of guilt. You are caught up with so many feelings about the shock of the condition, the ignorance of where it might lead, the anxiety, the pain from every treatment, the side effects, and the uncontrollable mental processes that take you from safe areas to places of total fear where your thoughts can be completely unreasonable. So I mainly sought validation of my anxiety and an assurance that others were mindful of my situation. Too much sympathy was not helpful because it made me feel I was losing something.

One of the therapists from whom I sought help, Larry, advised me to "visualize." He told me to see myself performing the activities I would carry out after the cancer was cured. A light went on in my mind and I thought, "I can easily do that." I am a master of these techniques and I had all the resources and tapes I needed. I started visualizing all kinds of good things. I saw the medicine as a beam of light passing through me to strike and destroy the disease, and I started picturing the days that would follow my healing. It was easy to do and kept my mind from wandering into unpleasant territory. This was one of the best pieces of advice I received.

The ultimate epiphany came from a verse in the Bible: "Trust in the Lord and try not to lean on your own understanding. In everything acknowledge Him and He will straighten your path." This theme anchored me all through my ordeal. The more I mulled it over, the stronger my inner mind became as I gathered my resources to face the road ahead.

What did I learn from my encounter with cancer and chemotherapy? First, the sense of panic is much worse than the actual physical illness. And a support system is essential. Emotional well-being is absolutely necessary for the repair and recuperation of the body. Modern medicine with its treatments, transplants, and supplemental therapies can help your physical body return to near normal. But after the fear and distress you have undergone, you will probably never be the same. It may be hard to regain your inner strength since at times floodgates can burst from trivial triggers.

At the same time, you learn to sync your mind and body much more tightly. The two form one continuum, and you realize it far more powerfully than you ever had before. You must have heard about yogis and other holy men talking about meditation and peace of mind. Everything you do on one side has a profound effect on the other. Plenty of rest, good food, and sleep are the essential ingredients I found necessary for proper recovery. The love and affection poured out to you nourishes the withering body and the tiring mind. My wife and daughter used to sit by my bedside and simply stroke my forehead several times, and it was like an intravenous infusion going straight to my subconscious mind. Someone cared for me, and I could peacefully close my eyes and snooze off to a place beyond my distress.

The physical and mental effects are beyond my ability to articulate. All I can say is that insecurity, my lifelong enemy and partner, controlled me foremost. The fear of death made me more and more aware of my life. I realized that I had to live day by day, without planning for tomorrow. Simply being alive was precious and I needed to do all I could to take care of the present, either through eating small portions of food, taking the right medication, having a bath, or trying to sleep. Every little moment made me aware that life is extraordinary.

Chapter 23

A Life-Threatening Procedure

With my lone, persisting tumor, the question became: Should I have a bone marrow transplant or wait to see whether chemotherapy had scarred the tumor and stopped its growth? Dr. Nathan was apprehensive about the risks of the procedure, but patiently explained the pros and cons. Dr. Fred Rosenfelt sent me to UCLA, the local teaching hospital, for recommendations. He consulted with Dr. Sandra Horning, an expert in lymphoma, and opinions were divided. Even some non-medical people discouraged me from undergoing a life-threatening procedure like a bone marrow transplant, since I looked reasonably well at the time.

"Bone marrow transplant" was not in my lexicon. Even after studying and training for many years and establishing a busy practice, the term did not mean much to me. But I recalled learning about bone marrow in medical school. We used to gaze at it under the microscope and it fascinated me. My professor used to say, "Bone marrow is the factory that produces blood cells." It has a wealth of stem cells, which can grow into white cells, red cells, or platelets. The white cells protect us from infection, the red ones carry oxygen to all organs in the body, and the platelets help the blood clot.

But the marrow also produces, and modifies, a whole bunch of immune system functions crucial for our defense against infection. We live in an ocean of bacteria and viruses, yet the everyday miracle of the immune system keeps us from most infections. The bone marrow adapts to sickness and well-being by increasing the right blood lines our body needs at the right time. Wiping out the marrow with high-dose chemotherapy and replacing it was therefore a serious process.

Dr. Nathan referred me to our tertiary care center on Sunset Boulevard for another opinion. There I met Dr. Peter Falk, a trim, tall, sharp-looking physician with curly hair, a thick mustache, and very prominent eyebrows. He greeted me and my wife, considered my case, and recommended the transplant. He described the procedure in detail. First, they would collect stem cells from my blood and freeze them. Then they would kill the tumor with very high doses of chemotherapy that would completely destroy my bone marrow. Finally, they would thaw the stem cells and put them back into me. It was a transplant from me to me (or in medical terms, an autologous peripheral blood stem cell transplant).

The risks and complications were as grave as anything a patient in a hospital bed could face. I was afraid to go through with this hazardous strategy and initially I opposed it. After the high-dose chemotherapy and radiation demolished my marrow and immune system, the new graft of stem cells could take time to settle in and the course back to normal life could be erratic.

But Dr. Falk felt I was a good candidate to benefit from the procedure. Jokingly he said, "We need to get you back to work and collect that generous pension we have in our organization."

Through my dark clouds of fear and burden, Dr. Falk sent a beam of hope to me. He was very persuasive. I looked at my wife's face. She had a reassuring smile. Though deep in her eyes I saw fear, I also saw optimism that the transplant might give me a new life. I looked at that smile and sensed in her heart all the confidence I needed to give permission to Dr. Falk. A series of phone calls to the transplant coordinator, family members, and friends started the procedure rolling for the next phase of my treatment.

When my oncologist suggested that I have a bone marrow aspiration — that is, a withdrawal of marrow— to see if I had any cancer cells in the bones, my memory returned to medical school days when we aspirated marrow from the breastbone. The procedure is fearful and gruesome. As the patient lies on the bed, the physician inserts a fair-sized needle into the breastbone, taking exceptional care not to thrust it past the sternum, since the heart lay just beyond. Nowadays doctors use the pelvic bone as it is easier, safer, and less frightening to the patient. My bone marrow test came back normal and it cleared me for the transplant.

To collect the cells needed for the transplant, the marrow should be able to churn out plenty of stem cells into the bloodstream on demand. I received special injections of Neupogen to increase the blood counts and get as many stem cells spilling into the peripheral circulation as possible. Then these cells are collected from the blood by a process called "apheresis."

The collection took place at the City of Hope, a renowned cancer center. Once again I had a Port-a-Cath for chemotherapy, but they needed a larger tube in my chest to gather and later transplant the stem cells, to infuse blood and medications, and to withdraw multiple blood samples almost every day for monitoring the blood counts. So Dr. Ashok Reddy removed the Port-a-Cath and inserted a bigger one called a triple lumen Hickman catheter.

Our cousin Geevy flew in from Florida and helped drive me to the apheresis center for the stem cell collection. He bought me new T-shirts to wear during my hospital stay. In addition, Bina, Vivek, Tara, and my neighbor Andy took turns driving me to the center. There, they connected me to a filtering device and my blood circulated through it to sieve out the stem cells, in a procedure similar to kidney dialysis. Collecting the stem cells didn't hurt, but the Neupogen injections to stimulate the marrow caused agonizing pain in the bones. I had to lie down tied to a machine for four hours every time I went for collection. I needed three sessions before they got enough stem cells for the transplant. The cells were labeled and frozen, ready for infusion back into me after my heavy-dose chemotherapy.

I had a choice between full-body radiation or targeted radioactive treatment: IV Zevlin. I chose the latter, since it was a new procedure and kept the rest of the body from receiving unnecessary radiation. Zevlin has two key parts. First, it uses monoclonal antibodies, that is, specially designed antibodies that can recognize and approach tumor cells. Second, each antibody has a radioisotope — a variant of an element that gives off radiation — attached to it. So when injected, it not only finds the tumor cells because of the antibody, but delivers localized radiation to destroy it. This pinpoint treatment reduces the damage to the whole body. This was the treatment I had predicted 16 years earlier!

Dr. Raubitschek was the nuclear medicine physician at City of Hope who took scans of my body, showed where my tumors were located, and pointed out that the medicine would target those cells specifically. Raubitschek is a storyteller. He has lots of tales for every patient and colleague he meets, and his personality is well-known at City of Hope. He told us that on September 11, 2001, he was in New York presenting a paper on Zevlin to the Food and Drug Administration and had to stop halfway through as they heard that some planes had crashed into The World Trade Center. He was trapped in New York and it took him five days to get back to California. He convinced me of the success of this new drug regimen, and the next day he injected Zevlin into me.

During this time my niece Leelamma and her husband Roy visited us from India. Since Leelamma and I had grown up together, she had plenty of stories to tell. She also made soups and special dishes and tried to distract me from my anxiety about the impending next step: the bone marrow transplant itself.

She was curious to know if the procedure involved any surgery. I told her it was as simple as a blood transfusion. However, I added, after destruction of the bone marrow, the body was highly prone to infection and the transplant was actually a rescue plan to restore marrow function quickly. The physician infused the stem cells into the blood and like microsubmarines they found their way to the bone marrow and got trapped in its mesh. There they started producing new blood cells. The marvel of human body function!

It all sounded simple, I told her, but there was an enormous problem. Once you have received the high-dose chemotherapy and radiation, your bone marrow is gone and you have no defense against any infection till your blood counts return to normal. So the recovery period during which the new cells implant is critical, and you receive antibiotic, antifungal, and antiviral medications throughout it. You also need frequent blood and platelet transfusions to maintain your counts. She understood the gravity of it, and tried to reassure me that the prayers of all our relatives were with me. She and her husband prayed for me a lot during their stay with us.

I was admitted to City of Hope on August 26, 2004. As the name suggests, patients have endorsed the City of Hope Hospital as *the* place to build hope and get cutting-edge treatment for cancer. It was in Duarte, 45 minutes from our home, and it catered to the special needs of cancer patients and their families. Kaiser referred their transplant patients to City of Hope because they had perfected the technique and had many years of experience in performing transplants. Kaiser transplant specialists were on staff to look after their own patients. There were small cottages on the campus where a family from out of town could stay and cook. Its Japanese garden and the rose garden were very soothing and patients could stroll around them if their blood counts were normal.

Geri, the nursing assistant, greeted us in the room and provided three plastic containers for nausea. The sight was not very pleasant but soon we realized that we needed all of them, as the nausea was intense. She told me not to brush my teeth with a regular toothbrush and gave me toothpick-like sponges instead. This would reduce the risk of infection. The hospital supplied soaps, shampoos, and towels. She also gave me a special mouth rinse to sooth the oral ulcers that can appear during treatment.

The dietitian walked in soon after and carefully explained how to choose food. I should eat only well-cooked food after the transplant, she said. The cafeteria was open from 6 am to 7 pm and I could order anything from the menu whenever I wanted. I didn't have to wait for a set mealtime.

The charge nurse came in and checked that the Hickman catheter was functioning well, and she flushed it with heparin to keep the tube open.

The room had a TV and telephone. A reclining chair was at one side for family members to sleep in. Bina and Vivek used it a lot, as they never allowed me to stay one day or night unattended. But even though you could stretch out full length on it, the chair was still uncomfortable and the constant interruptions of nursing staff to check vital signs and the beeping of alarms and the IV machine kept them awake most of the night.

Bina had her wardrobe hanging in the car down in the parking lot and she had to go to a common bathroom area to take a shower. Vivek had a different game plan. He carried all his needs in his backpack and brought his own reclining camp chair to park outside the room, where he read during the night as I slept. He acted like a sanitizing officer every time he came to relieve Bina. He cleaned anything that I might touch with anti-septic wipes, from doorknobs to telephone handles. He had a good sense of maintaining a sterile environment from his experience in a VA hospital during his high school days, when he used to dissect rabbits for experi-ments, as well as from his training as an emergency medical technician. He would wash his hands longer than many of the medical staff attend-ing me. He also screened all visitors to my room and instructed them to wash their hands and wear masks. He was so meticulous that one day Dr. Nathan came to visit me and Vivek, half-dazed from a rough night with me, stopped him and directed him to wash his hands. It took him a few seconds to realize that it was my own oncologist!

He did so much more. He was extremely thorough in checking that all the IV fluids were running properly and cross-checking my vital signs with nurses. He got the blood counts when it was time for reporting. He held me and kept me from tripping over my IV poles when I had to use the bathroom. He brought me DVD's in his backpack he thought that I would like. He turned on the music in the evening to lull me to sleep. Most nights he was next to me like a custodian. He sat near my bed in the recliner read-ing, listening to all the little noises I made, and watching for any display of my discomfort. Occasionally he watched TV with headphones so that he wouldn't disturb me.

Many times I wondered, "Is this the baby I used to carry and sing lullabies to? Is this the child I took to the parks and meadows, who would run around and wrestle with me and always say he'd won? Is this the boy I took for soccer practice and cheered on from sidelines at track and field events? Is this the boy I took for skiing lessons and taught karate?"

He had grown into a mature young man and now he was helping me get up from my bed and walking with me in the hospital corridor to strengthen my weakened muscles. Had the time come to pass the baton to my next generation? If so, I thanked God I had a son who was capable of handling any adverse situation.

Between Bina and Vivek I could turn up the morphine drip and forget all the difficulties of my treatment, knowing that their eyes were watching over me all the time. Did I need a morphine drip for my bone marrow transplant? Yes, of course. Ulcers developed in my tongue and throat, and the pain was intolerable. I could not even swallow my own saliva. My tongue looked like raw beef and my throat and lips were black from recurrent bleeding into the ulcers.

Luckily, modern medicine has good pain control methods. I had the "patient control analgesia" (PCA) regimen. That meant I had a steady stream of morphine running though my veins all the time, but for breakthrough pain I could add an extra dose by pressing a button on the IV pump. The pump had safety mechanism that locked up if I tried to dial more than four extra doses a day. In that event the doctor reviewed the dosage. Many days I was not shy about using the maximum amount, as the pain was devastating.

The dietitian and Bina tried their best to give me tasty shakes and high-calorie drinks. I chose morphine over the shakes and tried to forget about nutrition, as it was hard to swallow anything. Since I was totally incapable of keeping myself nourished through oral shakes and soups, my weight plummeted.

Dr. Falk started me on intravenous nutrition. As protocol dictated, he ordered total parental nutrition (TPN), a fluid scientifically calculated to provide the basic metabolic calories you need to maintain weight. It is mainly a high concentration of glucose with all multivitamins and minerals required for normal life. I received fat supplements on alternate days. It looked like milkshake, and I enjoyed watching it go into my veins. The staff closely monitored my electrolytes and liver functions, and changed the ingredients in the fluids daily according to the lab results.

Dr. Falk and his assistant Tina attended me daily. The day they infuse the stem cells is called Day 0 and they count upwards to see when the blood count comes up. For me, Day 0 was September 1, when the technician arrived in my room with the frozen stem cells. The bag was stiff like cardboard until he thawed it, when it looked like tomato soup. It was interesting to watch the nursing staff and the technician inspect labels to make sure I was getting *my own* stem cells. They matched the labels on each bag with the written order, which they then compared to my wristband, with each nurse calling off the names and numbers. It almost felt like a NASA launch with people repeating launch codes.

Tara was at my bedside with a video camera to record the event. Bina's Aunt Leela read from Psalms 139:13-14: "For you formed my inward parts, you wove me in my mother's womb. I will thank you, for I am fearfully and wonderfully made." She prayed and asked God's blessing on the infusion and the healing of my illness.

A small thought crossed my mind: These two little bags of stem cells were going to change my life and help me win my war against lymphoma? I watched the cells flow into my veins and all I could do was to pray silently for the engraftment of these cells to produce new marrow.

I felt new life was flowing into me. But halfway through the infusion, a knot formed in my stomach and I started vomiting as I never had before. And that was the pattern for many days for me.

The critical period is from the time of infusion till the stem cells graft and start producing new cells. Just as NASA engineers bite their knuckles when the spaceship goes around the moon and radio communication ceases for awhile, my family waited anxiously every day during this period for the blood counts.

The nurse took the blood at 3 am and Bina would stay awake till 4 am to see the results. The blood count was the growth signal that the bone marrow had grafted and was ready to produce blood cells. But it was like waiting for a seed to poke through the ground. Again and again the nurse came back shaking her head and showing us the printout: the count was still zero. We kept asking Dr. Falk, "How many more days before we see cells in the blood?" He reassured us that I was well within the time frame he had seen for marrow to graft and that we should stay calm.

Yet the days were very long and anxiety ruled us. The nights were darker than before and the sunrise seemed far away. The nursing staff took my temperature and blood pressure three times a day, but Bina checked my temperature 15 times a day by putting her hand on my chest under my shirt. Her hands felt very cold and I told her several times to rely on the nursing staff, but her concern compelled her to do so. She would often move her hands from my chest and rub my forehead for long stretches of time. I always felt her love for me and her care for my suffering, and I usually closed my eyes and tried to escape to a world of no pain.

Looking back, she was on duty 24 hours a day with so much to attend to and care for while trying to dispel the anxiety of the entire setting. She kept the communication lines open, as there were constant calls from relatives and friends from all over the world. She kept visitors engaged even though it cut through her rest time. She adhered to the motto "Smile though your heart is aching." Later she told me she used to sit in the parked car and cry aloud to let the sorrow melt down.

I needed her for frequent bathroom visits and all excretions had to be watched for blood and reported. She tucked in the bedsheets when I kicked them off in my sleep. I became very sensitive to cold and she brought an electric blanket for me to cling to. Feeding me was a challenge for her since all food tasted like sawdust. She tried different flavors and combinations, but I only seemed to tolerate yogurt-based food well, so I had small amounts of rice and yogurt for many days.

Waiting for the white cell count to return felt like waiting for a flower to bloom. Ten days passed and my WBC remained zero while my platelet count was around 6,000, instead of the normal 150,000-200,000.

Then I developed a fever of 104.

Dr. Neil Kogut was on call that night. He immediately realized that I had developed an infection in my blood through my Hickman catheter and he asked a surgeon to remove the device immediately. My logical mind said that if someone pulled a tube from such a big vein in my chest, I'd need a great many platelets to clot the wound or it wouldn't heal. Yet my platelet count was almost undetectable. The surgeon was concerned as well and he ordered transfusions of both platelets and blood. He also used the age-old technique of applying pressure on the wound and put a sand bag on my chest.

The culture came back in two days and it showed a fungal infection in my blood that originated in my catheter. Antifungal infusions were pre-scribed in consultation with the infectious disease department.

When they infused the first dose I told my son that my sight was blurry and I felt dizzy. He alerted the nursing staff immediately and later I real-ized that I had had an allergic reaction to the infusion. I was going into shock with very low blood pressure and I was turning blue from lack of oxygen. The timely intervention of the attending team pulled me out of this crisis after many hours.

However, the antifungal medicine took a toll on my kidneys. My tests started showing renal function failure and low potassium in the blood, as my kidneys were not balancing potassium normally. I received massive infusions for many days but the potassium level remained low.

The physicians were concerned but continued replacing the potassium I was losing. Bina sent word about my deteriorating kidney function to relatives in Seattle and a famous evangelist Mr. M.M. Zachariah, who was visiting from Kerala. Mr. Zachariah was a family friend for two generations and he had attended our wedding. Bina's grandfather, K.G. Thomas, was one of the founding fathers of the Brethren church in Kerala and Brother Zachariah was an associate of his. On that day he asked all our relatives to kneel down in the living room of Bina's uncle John Thomas and they prayed earnestly for divine intervention to restore my renal function.

The next day Bina was pacing the corridor to see if Dr. Falk was coming for rounds. She spotted Tina holding my lab results and Dr. Falk laughing in amazement at them. Seeing Bina, they beckoned her and told her that my potassium level was adequate and my kidney function normal.

Normal? It wasn't possible in so short a time, so they asked for a second sample. When the results came back identical, we all lifted our eyes upwards silently, acknowledging that there are indeed miracles in medicine.

The white blood count on Day 11 showed 100 cells per cubic millimeter. It was a good sign and we all knew that the stem cells had grafted in the marrow and started producing new cells. The count began rising each day, and to boost it Dr. Falk ordered a Neupogen injection to stimulate the marrow so that the count would be higher.

But even though the counts were going up, my body strength was going down. All transplant patients are supposed to take a shower no matter how tired they are, to wash away millions of bacteria that normally live on our skin. When the immune system is compromised you need to do all you can to keep the bacterial counts low.

But as I felt my strength slipping away from me, even the normal routines of life became burdensome. The physiotherapy staff came every day to help me do exercises. Even so, getting up from bed and standing in the shower was a herculean task and I could not do it without Bina's help. She spread towels on the bathroom floor so I wouldn't slip and she dialed the temperature to the right warmth. I always had to grab onto the bar in the bathroom to keep from falling.

I spent five weeks in the hospital, and it was a long slog. My body and spirit were lagging. Bina and the kids had had their lives scrambled to accommodate my needs. Yet my stay at the City of Hope left indelible memories. The nursing staff provided exceptional care and we truly felt hope that the cancer was contained. The biggest challenge to the attending team was to stabilize my nutritional status and maintain my body weight.

Finally, the day arrived for my discharge from the hospital. As I left, Dr. Falk threatened that they would readmit me if I lost even two pounds.

Back at home, I was hardly out of danger. The first hundred days after the transplant are crucial for preventing infections and monitoring blood-work for complications. To keep the bacterial counts low, all my food had to be cooked fresh and could not be reheated in the microwave. I couldn't eat raw vegetables or fruits at all, and I absolutely had to avoid crowds. Bina's meticulous planning and the children's untiring assistance helped me get through those days.

I saw Dr. Falk on follow-up at his clinic three times a week initially and then twice a week. Once he saw that I did not need many transfusions and infusions of potassium and magnesium during my clinic visits, he asked me to see him in his office at the Kaiser Sunset facility.

I attended Thanksgiving dinner at the home of our cousins Sunny and Kunjumol, and we hosted Christmas dinner. With a thankful heart to God for seeing us through such a stormy year we welcomed January 2005.

CHAPTER 24

The Digital Changeover

On January 13, 2005, I got a call from our department chief, Dr. Ramanathan. He asked how I was spending my time and I said I was reading and working on my computer. He asked whether I might like to join a group that was planning to make medical records digital.

I had a reputation for computer skill on campus. Over the years I had contributed in this area, and I had also belonged to the steering committee for information technology. The department and the medical center felt a little unsure about the whole paper-to-bytes program and they wanted someone with the drive and know-how to ease the transition. After discussions with the clinical content coordinator, Dr. Erin Stone, I joined the team representing all the Kaiser medical centers in Southern California.

I felt it was an important assignment. Most other industries had already taken advantage of the digital recordkeeping technology, but medical records had been stuck with pen and paper. Thus when I saw a patient and sent him or her for tests, the nurse had to fill out a stack of forms, labeling and check-marking them, and handing them over to the patient. He or she then took them to the lab. If the patient stopped for a bathroom break, he might lose a paper. At the lab, the receptionist would transfer all the information to the system in the department and give the patient an appointment or do the test immediately.

With electronic medical records, I knew we could replace all those steps with a single click. After I saw a patient, I would simply choose tests from a pull-down menu and this information would go at once to different departments already prioritized and categorized. No one would have to re-enter it or try to decipher the tests I had ordered. The system also sent automatic alerts about duplicate tests, saved time and money for the institution, and prevented unnecessary procedures for the patient. And it utterly transformed prescription writing. Computerized records cut down errors and accurately spelled out instructions for the pharmacist and the patient. The patient enjoyed the convenience of going to any pharmacy for processing, and didn't have to carry around and possibly lose a piece of paper.

Moreover, even though different departments had mini-systems, I found it exciting that we would centralize the whole patient care function on a single platform. The pharmacy, billing, laboratory, radiology, and all other departments would operate from one hub. It would cut down on needless effort and errors.

Despite these benefits, most people (except for a few physicians and the program managers) saw the arrival of digital records as a tsunami. They felt comfortable with the age-old tradition of pen and paper and the chart that physically followed the patient around. Though illegibility was a common complaint and records were often hard to access, medical personnel were unwilling to shift to a system where they sat at a computer to enter information cleanly and where they could easily view data from anywhere. Beyond the general resistance to change, some people genuinely worried about their typing and computer skills. The people in my department knew my computer skills but also thought I could reassure my colleagues as they faced the uncertain, unpleasant, and inevitable change.

My motto was: Embrace any change for the good. I have seen so many upheavals in my life. I remember my residency, when I felt ignorant since I had never struck a typewriter key or even seen a computer. My fellow residents used these devices easily while I had to rely on the department secretary to help me type my thesis and papers. I saw the advantages of this technology, enrolled in all the evening computer classes, mastered many programs, and became very comfortable with computers.

I had also never seen or used a pager till my early years in residency. I remember the early days, when I was on call. The call would come to the physician in the "call book." The nurse might write in the book, "Bed number 15 has a fever. Please come see the patient." She would give it to the orderly on the floor, who would track down the physician or meet him at his call room. The physician on call would acknowledge the message by signing it and prioritize his visit according to the number of patients he had to attend. So when I first saw the pager, I thought it was a great idea, since it eliminated the orderlies' trips, reduced paperwork, and brought doctors to patients' bedsides faster. Similarly, when cell phones came into extensive use, communication speeded up.

To me this assignment was a God-given opportunity. It fed into my lifelong appreciation of change. I knew it would be exciting to see the switch from paper to electronic medical records. And though I couldn't deal directly with patients because of the risk of infection, I could throw my energies into the program and help out my medical center.

I quickly realized that digitization would not be a tsunami at all, but rather a series of small waves from department to department as we networked the program. I saw that with proper preparation and training we could do it well.

I set to work. First, I went through the huge list of common tests and medications one could order through a computer system. The challenge was enormous, as we had to proceed line-by-line. Things became more interesting once we started looking at the order sets. Order sets are preprogrammed groups, essentially templates. For example, if I admitted a patient with chest pain, with one click I could bring up all the orders that the patient needed, such as oxygen therapy, nitroglycerine, pain control and beta blockers, EKG, alerts to cardiology, aspirin, and many others, customizable for each patient. There was consensus and approval from all the representatives from the region in this regard and we followed the guidelines set by the corresponding American Board specialty.

The administrative staff had few problems changing over. But the clinical staff resisted, as they were used to the old ways, and during lunch periods, they often talked about their anxieties. I gave many lectures and hands-on lessons to colleagues to help alleviate their fears. The surgeons wondered how we would schedule all the operating room events on a computer. The emergency room staff were concerned that records might not reflect the complexity and speed of their bed and physician changes in the ER (the conventional method was a chalkboard which showed patients' movements from room to room). The social workers and psychiatrists were apprehensive about the security and confidentiality of the charts.

But the administrators and programmers understood the advantages of a centralized, integrated system that would streamline and accelerate patient care. For instance, the radiology department would have instant access to services the patient received at, say, the outpatient clinic, ER, or pharmacy. Or to any services they received anywhere before the paper record of them arrived and entered the computer.

The launch took place department by department in our campus. Billing went first, then pharmacy. The clinical side was the big challenge, as we had to plan the patient load and training for the MDs. After a month of training, on the week of launch we cut the patient load in half to get physicians and nurses familiar with the new system. Gradually, we increased the load as the staff grew more at ease. I was able to help many of them, one-on-one and collectively, adapt to the new way of documenting patient care.

After four weeks most of the physicians were comfortable writing notes and ordering tests and medications on the computer. The providers started to like the convenience of the access to charts anywhere, any time. And I felt good and kept busy. I felt productive and useful again.

CHAPTER 25

Gold Mine in the Back Yard

A cassette tape ignited my curiosity.

In childhood, my nephew Raju and I were notorious adventurers. He was with me when the elephant chased us to his uncle's house. He was also with me when we narrowly escaped drowning while playfully bathing in Pamba River near my sister's house in Ranni. We stayed in the same hostel in college, swam in the canals of Tiruvalla for many hours, and played hockey for the college team.

Over the years we had lost touch with each other as we were busy building our own careers, as it was before the age of easy telephone communications and the Internet.

Fast-forward 30 years. One day I got a letter from my sister saying that Raju had retired from Oman and was taking Bible classes in her church. I called my sister Molly and asked for details. She said he was teaching from the Book of Revelation and his classes were excellent.

Teaching from the Book of Revelation? My curiosity grew. That book is full of vivid images and symbolism. Many Bible teachers hesitate to touch it as there are many interpretations and conclusions in that book.

I called Leelamma, Raju's sister, and asked if she had any cassette tapes from Raju's Bible teaching. She sent me one with the handwritten title "Song of Songs, Bible class by John P. Thomas (Raju)."

I could not control my thoughts. He was teaching Revelation and now was taking classes on the Song of Songs. Couldn't he just stick with creation stories and the Gospels? I grew up in a family where reading sexually related material was discouraged and my boarding school training made me feel guilty if I gazed at a magazine with any sexual overtones. But I used to read the Song of Songs in boarding school, as we were permitted to read the Bible. I read it mainly to see the description of a bride and the passion of love. Since it was Biblical, nobody could fault me.

Raju had studied in the same boarding school and I asked myself, "What happened to him?" Why was he deviating from the values we learned there: avoid sexual literature and read more scientific or historical materials instead?

With mixed feelings I put the cassette in my stereo system and started listening. I was mesmerized by his opening remarks that the Song of Songs had no sexual content and it was all about God's love reflected in human feelings. He went through that book describing the love of God to Israel as many Jewish scholars do and the love of Christ to the church as many Christians do. He satisfied my curiosity about why the Bible, which deals with God, had to have a narrative about human sexuality. His ability to explain the poetic language, the spiritual symbolism hidden in these lines, and their meaning for Christian life was amazing. I was spellbound by his knowledge of the scripture and his ability to express it in depth.

The tape stirred me to study the Bible and I started reading the Song of Solomon for its spiritual message: "He has brought me to his banquet hall, and his banner over me is LOVE." I realized that it is a mystical book with a historic basis as Solomon penned it, using Middle Eastern imagery and poetry. But its spiritual content was beyond my thoughts.

Raju (John P. Thomas) is now a leading Bible teacher in Kerala. He has traveled through many parts of the world, including the United States, preaching and teaching from the Bible. His expository manner with sermons is very popular in Kerala and abroad. Thus my nephew instigated in me the love of studying the Bible.

But the question arose: How was I going to study this Bible, which is such a difficult book to comprehend? There is a saying in India: "When the student is ready, the teacher appears." That is what happened to me next.

"Found the gold mine" is a phrase everyone understands. In my spiritual journey I have explored all means for fostering internal peace and sanity in life. Certainly, feeding the mind with outstanding material bears good fruit. In spite of my busy schedule, I always took time to sharpen my wisdom and pursue more knowledge by whatever avenue I could. I had read the Bible all my life, but it was like nibbling. I perused a little bit here and a little bit there. I went over daily devotional readings, and I occasionally became inspired by a sermon and read material relating to it.

But I had never tried to study the Bible completely. I know I can claim lack of time, saying that I work day and night with my medical practice. However, intellectually I knew that scripture reading was the only way to increase knowledge, and increased knowledge yields obedience in life. Obedience in turn yields holiness and holiness nourishes further spiritual growth.

From childhood I knew from the Bible that prayer was important in my spiritual journey. My parents instilled in me the need for daily prayer. When I woke up early in the morning, I heard my father praying with my mother in their bed for all the children and for their future. We had family prayer before we ate, slept, or did anything special. So I had no problem adapting to prayer, as my needs and wants seemed far greater than I could satisfy. I prayed for everything: good grades in school, protection of my family, a wife suitable to me, good health for my children, and provisions in life. Prayer was a spiritual discipline and pattern in my life. It kept me humble and dependent on God for everything.

I have now lived in four different countries and seen many ways of life, including a variety of spiritual habits and worship styles. I have attended churches and worshiped God all over the world. I have prayed in famous cathedrals such as Westminster Abbey in London, Notre Dame in Paris, and Cologne Cathedral in Germany. I have prayed to God atop the Alps in Switzerland and on the steps of the Sydney Opera House. My personal prayer life was sound and continuous.

But I still felt a stab of sadness that I didn't spend as much time studying the Word of God as my father would have wished. Would it affect my spirituality and my reward in heaven? That was a big question and I did not have the answer to it. I longed for a place where I could quench my thirst for spiritual growth.

One day my cousin Sunny visited me from Canada. He said there was a preacher in California named John MacArthur whom he listened to on the radio while he commuted. Sunny wanted to visit his church and see him in person.

I had never heard of this preacher and I said I would search the Internet to find the site of his church. Lo and behold, it was two blocks from my hospital in Panorama City. I had seen big crowds and parking congestion when I drove through that area on Sundays, but I had always ignored the commotion. We have a saying in diagnostic medicine: "The eyes do not see what the mind does not know."

I realized that John MacArthur was one of the most influential preachers of this time and his teaching and ministry went out to all parts of the world. He has a study Bible available in English, German, Russian, Spanish, and Italian. Arabic and Chinese translations are also forthcoming, and will reach millions around the globe.

Wow! I had been looking for knowledge and spiritual growth, and here was a gold mine. The "student is ready and the teacher is in my back yard." I attended his church, listened to his sermons, bought many of his books, and started enjoying a different level of scripture learning. I have attended evening classes at his seminary, Logos Bible Institute, to study the whole Bible and internalized his study Bible. I have now listened to hundreds of his tapes on different theological aspects of Christianity.

It was a herculean task for me to keep up with the Bible study while juggling my daily work and evening calls. Over the course of two years, I often finished seeing patients at the clinic, threw my white coat and stethoscope into the trunk of my car, and rushed to attend classes from 6 to 10 pm, without a proper dinner. Added to that, the homework and extra reading to catch up with the class threw me back to my medical school days, where my routine was work, study, and sleep — and nothing else.

My family was very supportive, and understood my passion and focus. Tara used to say, "Dad, why do you have five books open when you are studying the Bible? How many Bibles do you have now?"

I fell in love with the Bible I had in my desk from school days till now. I had studied volumes of medical books and most of them have been updated, corrected, and reprinted. But the Bible is the same all over the world. The same thoughts inspired by divine deliberation written by 40 authors over a period of 1500 years. It is impossible for man to produce such a manuscript which does not contradict but rather supplements itself.

Bible study became an ongoing intellectual contemplation for me, a process. The Bible was an emotional escape and a sacred book I carried to the church on Sundays for many years of my life. When I sat down in a classroom to study it, the richness captivated me. It was intellectually challenging, emotionally gratifying, and spiritually enriching. It had everything I needed for spiritual growth.

The mind of God is revealed in the words of inspired people. The study of cosmo-centric creation of the heavens, the geocentric creation of Earth followed by bio-centric creation of life in land, sea, and air, and finally the anthro-centric creation of man described in the beginning of the Bible eased my intellectual concerns regarding evolution. Archeologists have verified the histories it depicts. The music and psalms penned by King David gave me vocabulary and melody to express my emotions. The study of Proverbs was like going to business school, learning what to do and what not to do. My blind faith started yielding to a way to search and find answers in the Bible. I knew that if I read it I would be wise and if I practiced it I would be holy. I had a gold mine in my back yard and I drew from that mine.

Over the years my knowledge escalated and my faith and spirituality deepened. Knowledge typically breeds arrogance, but Bible knowledge brings humility and love to one's life, and I enjoyed that aspect of it more than the wisdom I acquired. I thought I had unshakable faith and spirituality, but God put me into a crucible where my faith and spirituality were tested.

I completed my course at Logos in September 2003, two months before my cancer diagnosis. After I became ill, many people asked me, "How was your spiritual journey? Did you become more spiritual after your sickness?" With the cancer, I suddenly found myself in a state of helplessness. I felt frustration, anger, and self-pity. I became a prisoner of all my fears. I was emotionally raw and vulnerable. I was in shock and in my suffering I felt alienated. I did not want people to see me physically weak and withering away. I was afraid of dying a horrible death from cancer. I needed assistance to keep from falling into deep depression. I often asked myself, "What happened to my faith?" I felt it slipping away from me as fear dominated my emotions.

Yet when crisis engulfed me, my prayer grew more intense, vigorous, and urgent. Prayer was the main tool I personally had and it became an experience more than a request. At the same time, the love and devotion of my family were powerful enough to fight this state of mind, with the help of prayers from many people. I had professional help to see me through these tough times, but the unconditional love from Bina, Vivek, and Tara gave me hope and healed my troubled spirit.

CHAPTER 26

From the Taj to Tiruvalla

W hen Bina makes breakfast for me, I sit in the breakfast nook and read the newspaper. We usually talk about past events or projects ahead of us. One day I was reading about India's prosperity in the business section of the paper and I grew nostalgic. We had not seen India for 14 years, as none of our parents were still alive, but we had heard much about its vibrant new economy.

Bina pushed the paper aside and placed an omelet and sausage in front of me. She brought me a cup of tea, moved all my morning medicine closer to the tea, and sat down beside me.

I suggested that we take a trip to India. Two years had passed since the bone marrow transplant. My immune system was back to near normal. My blood counts and CT scan were normal. It seemed like a good time to return.

I have brothers and sisters there, but Bina's only brother died at 28 and her ties to India had greatly diminished. I told her that it would be nice to see her brother's son Unni, who now lived with his mother and step-father in Chennai (Madras), as well as her devoted nanny Nandini. I saw a sparkle in her eyes. Nandini had come to work for Bina's parents when Bina was six, and had been the caretaker for the family all her life. When we got married I came to know her better. She is petite, barely five feet tall.

She is also loyal, sincere, and very caring. She had been with the family during its ups and downs. Bina's parents were busy with the publication of the newspaper and weekly, and Nandini managed the household chores with no difficulty. I typically saw her in the kitchen preparing meals for us, and she could multitask by answering phone calls while putting away the laundry and tidying up the house. She took care of our son Vivek for six months before he joined us in England, and she kept the household going when Bina's mother passed away, looking after her father and Unni. There was no way to repay her devotion to the family with money and for Bina, Nandini was not a servant or nanny, but a friend and a big sister. We agreed to visit her and make sure that she had a good place to stay. I needed nothing more to convince Bina to go to India.

As we were speaking, Tara came in, sat in the chair next to me, and asked what we were talking about. I told her that I hadn't seen India for a long time and now that I was feeling physically well it would be nice if she came with us to visit our family back there.

Tara is a family person. She keeps careful track of all birthdays and pores over family photos constantly. She was born in England but had gone to India when she was a month old and then joined me in Canada two months later. She had stayed with us throughout her schooling, including college. Now she showed a spark of interest in joining us for the trip.

Tara turned to Bina and asked, "What kind of clothes can I wear in India?" Bina explained to her that India was now very modern and she could wear pants, blouses, and skirts. Bina was also fond of Indian salwar kameez (loose, pajama-like trousers together with a long shirt) and assured Tara that she would buy attractive Indian garments for her.

"So where will we stay in India?" Tara asked.

I told her that we had extended family in India and would stay with different cousins and relatives every day. Knowing full well that she was of marriageable age, I got her attention by asking her, "Can I look for a suitable match for you while we are in India?"

She turned her chair towards me and replied, "How can I marry someone I don't know?"

She had heard our story many times in bits and pieces, but now I repeated that though I had not known her mother before I married her, we had been together for over 30 years. She wanted to hear the story of our marriage again and I thought it was a good time to explain arranged marriage in general.

Like a professor lecturing a class, I began by saying it was like Internet dating in this country, except the parents did the background check, since they knew us well and tried to find the perfect match. The parents looked at religion, educational status, and social level of each party. When compatibility seemed likely, the couple met in the presence of the parents and later could express their individual feelings about the proposal. Statistically, arranged marriage works much better than "love" marriage in Western society.

"But what did you have in common?" Tara asked.

I explained that I was a 25-year-old doctor and Bina had finished her master's degree in chemistry. We both belonged to the same church and our grandfathers knew each other. When they looked at us they thought we would make a happy couple as we both were educated and had a good family background.

Arranged marriage can work because the parents match the basics in life and then the couple has the responsibility to make it grow. You pour love and respect into the marriage and it will work. And since it is a union between two families, the partners have a common interest in making it succeed. You don't have to go searching for a common interest, and in any case once children arrive there is no need to hunt for one.

Even though she did not seem enthusiastic, Tara was clearly curious about her cultural background and we decided to book our tickets to India.

An Air France carrier took us to Paris in the last week of November 2006, and we stayed in Paris for two days. Since our children didn't remember their previous European trip, we took a car and driver and explored Paris. The Eiffel Tower was magnificent, the Louvre was colorful and enriching, and Notre Dame Cathedral was extraordinary.

The next leg of our journey took us to New Delhi, the capital of India. The touchdown was very emotional for me, since there had been times when I wasn't sure I would ever see my motherland again. Shibu, my niece Jessy's husband, met us in the airport and took us to his house. A chauffeur-driven van was arranged for our transportation in Delhi. Nandini joined us from Kerala, and Bina and the children were very excited to see her after many years.

After casual sightseeing in the city, we decided to go visit the most beautiful building in the world: the Taj Mahal. The drive down to Agra was memorable. We had left India over a decade ago and the traffic had now swelled to the point that it could come to a standstill whenever a cow or a bullock cart crossed the road. The bleating of horns was irritating at first, but then the reality set in that we were now in a different country and we started accepting it.

The driver had his radio tuned in to local Hindi stations and I enjoyed the songs. Tara and her cousin Ammu, who joined us in Delhi, were listening to an iPod from a single earphone and mouthing the words in sync. Bina and I soaked up all the sights on the wayside.

We stopped at Fatehpur Sikri, a magnificent historical city built by the emperor Akbar as the capital of his Mughal empire. It was later abandoned and now the palace and tombs are tourist attractions. On the way we passed through small villages with sheep and cows wandering around and children playing in the canals. We guessed that foreign visitors would find the scene colorful but be surprised by the low standard of living near one of the marvels of the world. At the city itself, we took photos, visited some of the inner structures, and saw beautiful carvings, pillars, and building stones that would compel anyone's attention, even without knowledge of history or help from a guide.

Then we headed to Agra. We checked in at the Taj Hotel, freshened up, and prepared to see the Taj Mahal. Shibu suggested that we hire a guide from the hotel to make our tour easy and pleasant, and it proved a good idea.

We had to park far away from the Taj and we took a horse-drawn car-
riage to approach it. There, we saw the long line of people waiting for a
ticket to get in. Our guide said he knew the back entrance and led us on a
walk through narrow gullies flowing with dirty water. We tiptoed our way
to the lonely back entrance. Even it was crowded by any normal standard,
but we moved pretty quickly through the lines and got our tickets.

I had visited the Taj before, and we all had seen pictures of this univer-
sally admired, white-domed miracle in marble. Yet once we crossed the
main gate and viewed it over the multitude of tourists, it took our breath
away. We inched our way to the building and took many photos from different angles. The beauty of the Mughal garden, the reflecting pool, the
calligraphy on the pillars, and the other fine details on the structure itself is
beyond any poet's ability to describe and all I can say is: See it and believe.
And then blot away the beauty and understand the grief of the builder
Shah Jahan for his beloved, deceased wife Mumtaz, who inspired him to
create this epic in stone.

Our next destination was Hyderabad. This populous city in Andhra
Pradesh is now the hub of India's Information Technology Institutes. Bina's
cousin Sara is married to Brigadier Ipe, and he met us at the airport. As
we greeted each other, I was seeing the brigadier for the first time. He led
us to the baggage claim area and we quickly realized the power of his uniform. He was the commanding officer of the regiment in Hyderabad, and
the military personnel accompanying him helped us find our way through
the baggage claim.

With escort cars before and behind us, we reached his residence. It was
an old British colonial-style mansion with many rooms, servants' quarters, guard post, well-kept lawn, and an array of servants to attend to his
needs. We basked in the perks of his rank and enjoyed all the hospitality
Sara offered us. Since we were still jetlagged, we went to our bedrooms
and rested well.

Hyderabad is famous for diamonds and precious stones, so the next day
we drove out to shop in the Charminar area, at a monumental, square,
four-towered building in the heart of the city. As soon as we opened the

car door, beggars stretched out their hands to us. Bina unlatched her bag and gave them money. Within minutes, a mob of them was following us and we needed help from the local people to get them to leave us alone. The residents know that if you show beggars a little sympathy they will squeeze you, and so have developed a callousness about the woeful faces and open palms in the shopping area. We saw plenty of bright stores filled with beautiful bangles, scarves, and jewelry. We also visited the Qutub Shahi tombs built in 1671 with their marvelous stonework and gardens.

That evening we dined at the officers' mess. The army band greeted us and soldiers had erected special tents to enhance the experience, and we spent the evening in a relaxed atmosphere.

Next day we visited the Golkonda fort built in 1600s. Golkonda is believed to be the excavation site of the famous Koh-i-noor diamond. Vivek and Tara ventured to climb up the fort with their cousins, while Bina and I stayed in the gardens socializing with the soldiers from the Punjab regiment. At sunset we saw the light and sound show and of course we had front row seats because of the brigadier and his first lady.

Early next morning we boarded a flight to Chennai (called Madras when I lived in India), where Unni and his mother Shirley welcomed us. Unni was a baby when we left the country and now he was a young man six feet tall. Bina hugged her nephew as if he were her deceased brother. Tara and Vivek hadn't seen him for years and so they had a lot of catching up to do. My nostalgia was rising as I was getting close to my home state.

We traveled to Kerala by Kingfisher Airlines, one of the new private carriers that competed with government-run Indian Airlines. We had rarely flown in India before we left years ago, and we were pleased to see that the service on the ground and onboard was very pleasant and efficient. As the plane descended into Kochi, we saw feathery-fronded coconut palms stretching for miles and miles, as well as thick green rubber trees and a mosaic of paddy fields. Many Keralites are proud of their beautiful land and call it God's own country.

My older brother Philip met us and took us to his house, where we ate a classic Kerala breakfast of tapioca, duck egg roast, and appam (pancakes) with chicken stew.

Then we set off on the drive to Tiruvalla, and I saw how much change had come to my homeland. The traffic was a nightmare, with far more motor vehicles on the same narrow roads. The paddy fields and coconut trees sharpened my nostalgia, but I was nervous all the way as our driver maneuvered through congestion. We stopped briefly at Union Christian College at Alwaye, where I had studied for one year before entering medical school, and I showed my kids the campus and the hostel where I had stayed.

By evening we reached Tiruvalla. Johnychayan (Dr. John Joseph) and his wife Elsy opened their luxurious home for us and we had a refreshing day of rest. Johnychayan was a dear cousin to me and a role model, as he was the first one from our family to go to dental college. He had given me lots of good advice during my career and gotten me into the internship program at Trivandrum Medical College.

Next morning my older sister Lillykochamma and our longtime servant Bhavani came to see us. Lillykochamma had wanted to see me for years and I could feel her joy in the tightness of her hug. We cried and laughed at the same time since she was so glad to set eyes on me after my cancer ordeal. She was happy to see Vivek and Tara as grown up adults. Bhavani is the servant who stayed with my mother for 19 years when she was widowed. She looked half as big as I remembered and she broke out in tears seeing me. She sat on the floor rubbing my feet and crying. I did not know what to say to her, but I remembered all the love and loyalty she had for our family. Her service was priceless and her companionship to my mother during her lonesome days had been invaluable.

I had not been able to attend my mother's funeral, so I asked Lillykochamma to take me to the cemetery where she was buried. We sat down at the gravesite and I could not hold back my tears. I burst into a loud cry. Lillykochamma put her arms around me and reminded me that she had died in peace after a long, contented life. She added that Mother was very happy that I was well-settled in America, and that she appreciated all the financial help and emotional pleasure I had given her till the end. I felt I had closure as I wept for my mother at her final resting place.

That day we also attended a wedding of my cousin Josekuttychayen's daughter. (Josekuttychayn was the cousin who had enthralled me as a child with bedtime stories of princes and princesses when we stayed with my maternal grandfather.) We met many of our relatives and family members and enjoyed a typical Kerala-style wedding feast.

On the way back to Johnychayan's I asked the driver to stop in front of the two-story home my father built in 1958, near downtown Tiruvalla. As the younger son, by tradition I had inherited the property. Since I had settled in Los Angeles, my brother Philip bought it from me and our mother continued living there until her death in 1995. A year before my trip Philip had sold the property, and even though it was sad for me and other family members, I understood that it was not practical for him to keep up two homes in two different cities.

Now I saw that the front courtyard was clean and the house seemed newly painted. But the post at the gate was blank where it had once displayed our family name THAMARASSERIL on a plaque. The big shady mango tree I used to climb next to the gate had vanished, and the giant jackfruit tree which produced the tastiest fruit in that area was also gone.

I wanted to see the inside of the house again, so I knocked on the door. The host greeted our family and we sat down in the living room. Bina kept the conversation going, but my mind lapsed into a series of flashbacks. This was the house where I spent most of my formative years in middle school and part of high school. This was the house our family called home, the hub for all family visits. This was the house where I woke up in the morning next to my parents' bedroom, hearing them pray for the well-being and blessings for all their children. This was the house where I recuperated after my train accident, the house where I came on my holidays from my medical school to be pampered by mother and relax like a cat, the house where I sat on the porch for hours watching the cars and people pass by and dreaming big about my future. This was the house where, when I walked in with my medical degree, I saw the proudest parents on earth. This is the house where I brought my beautiful bride Bina to start my new stage of life. This was the house where Vivek used to run around and proudly say, "This is Appa's (Dad's) house." This was the house where I had seen my father sitting on the veranda with his feet up reading the Bible for hours. This was the house where my mother and father lived together after their retirement. And this was the house where they both said good-bye to this world after raising six children.

As the hostess walked in with refreshments for us, I blinked a few times to bring myself out of the daze. I don't remember much of the conversation as nostalgia and emotions still filled my mind. I was ready to open the floodgates and burst into tears.

CHAPTER 27

My Hometown in the 21st Century

From the outset I had planned a trip back to Mallapally, my birth-place. I wanted to show Vivek, Tara, and Bina my school, my neighborhood, and the river where I learned to swim. My brother Philip came with us. As we neared it I tried to recall some of the land-marks, and Philip confirmed them as he had visited the town several times.

First, we visited the primary school. The old thatched building was now fully tiled. The road I used to run along with such fear was paved and cars could easily drive it. And on our former property now stood a new house built closer to the roadside. The vegetation was completely changed, with big rubber trees and other crops.

I took my family down to the river. It was smaller than I recalled, and it sounded and even smelled different. The roaring, rough, majestic wa-terway had shriveled to half its size, and the old washing stone once sur-rounded by three or four ladies cleaning clothes now stood abandoned. Where I had long ago savored the hustle and bustle of the people using the river for many reasons, I now saw just a lonely bather who waded in with his towel on his shoulder and a soap dish in his hand. We talked to him and could connect our family roots. He said that dams upstream and the scooping of sand for construction work had transformed the stream.

I used to race down the bank and splash joyfully into this river, but now I had to hold on to my brother to walk down to its edge. The place I had seen so often as a youngster looked altered in many ways, even through the trifocal transitional lens I was wearing. But Bina and the kids had images now for the stories they have heard about my childhood.

Lillykochamma had arranged a family reunion to celebrate my visit at her home in Ranni. About 35 people gathered there on a Sunday afternoon. Her daughters Leelamma and Rejini arrived two days before to help her, and her son Raju the previous day. As I mentioned earlier, Lillykochamma is famous for her hospitality and this time it was at its peak.

She had had servants brought in from neighborhood to set up a special kitchen in the courtyard, and we saw smoke rising from there as we drove into her compound. They had slaughtered a lamb and prepared a feast of almost Biblical proportions. As she greeted and gathered all of us together, she instructed the servants about the courses of the feast. She had goat biriyani, among other dishes, and this meal was the best we had had in years.

Lillykochamma's son Raju (John P. Thomas) had become a famous evangelist and he said now was a good time to give thanks to God and to hear from me about the healing mercies I had received from Him. We sang hymns and I gave my testimony and thanked the family for praying for me. Many family members thanked God for the grace He had showered on us and asked for His blessings in our future.

Just when we thought we had enough food the desserts arrived. Lillykochamma had brought in a special chef and he prepared payasam and pradaman. I had enjoyed Lillykochamma's feasts before, but this one was unforgettable for Bina and my children and they talk about it every time they recall our trip to India.

We celebrated my 57th birthday in Kumarakam and Vembanad Lake, which had become a well-known tourist destination. Among those who came with us were Lillykochamma, Johnychayan and his wife Elsykochamma from Tiruvalla, and my brother Philip, his son Manu and his daughter Leena, along with her husband and son. I had been to Kumarakam when I was a student and had crossed the lake on ferryboats. Its natural beauty had not changed, but the rise of tourist infrastructure in Kerala now made it more enjoyable and relaxing for anyone who wanted to spend a day or two there.

The trip from Kottayam to Kumarakam took 20 minutes. There we saw the thatched roof and coir-reinforced houseboats called *kettuvallam* docked at the lakeside. They can carry 15 to 30 people, depending on their size, and they had become the standard transportation for tourists. We rented one for the whole day. Three crewmembers greeted us and we boarded by climbing a slanted plank, as proper docking stations were still unavailable. The vessel had a spacious seating area for about 20 people, with chairs and benches on the edges, an air-conditioned bedroom, modern flush toilet bathroom, and a cooking area. Tara and Vivek had no idea what they were getting into, so they took out their iPods and listened to their favorite songs.

We pulled away from the shore. Thick trees shaded the narrow waterway on both sides and we passed a few boats coming in. The crew gave us lemon juice spiked with ginger and sugar, a refreshing beverage. As we emerged onto the open lake we saw small houses on the shore. The water was clean, blue, and tranquil. The boat left no ripples or wake, but just slid over the glassy surface, now and then cutting through floating vegetation. Vivek started looking at birds that were waiting for fish. Tara was playing with Aaron, my niece Leena's six-year-old son.

Even though we had grown up here, we never paid attention to the hidden treasures in our backyard. Now the beauty of the lake struck us as if we had never seen it before. Coconut trees lined the lake and blocked the horizon. We saw a lonely church on the shore, and passed a resort where tourists stay nowadays, with a beach and other recreational facilities. Certain views were like magical pictures we had seen on canvas paintings. A poet or travel journalist would revel in what we saw, but even with my scientific mind I enjoyed the serenity of this getaway right in my own land.

When the boat neared the shore, urchins and crowds waved at us. One crewmember asked me whether we were interested in locally made toddy (liquor from the coconut tree). Since we weren't, he steered his way through the stretch of islands and shorelines.

At lunchtime we docked near an embankment, where little boats crisscrossed back and forth and birds flocked to catch fish. There they served us first-class Kerala biriyani, with fried fish the size of a fist and coconut water. Even though the biriyani did not equal Lillykochama's, she agreed that it was of the highest caliber. Nandini, who can make five different types of biriyani, nodded in approval of its quality.

We never dreamed that tourist services had reached this level and we congratulated the head cook on his skills. He came back with the traditional payasam for dessert. Babuchayen had brought a cake with him. Everyone sang "Happy Birthday" to me, and then we cut and ate it.

After lunch we glided across the vast lake gazing at the lush green shores with their swooping coconut palms. All of us felt a little sleepy, and the soft music wafting from hidden speakers made it harder for us to keep our eyes open and absorb the splendor of Vembanad Lake.

Around four o'clock the crew brought us traditional tea with ginger and cardamom, and all of us found renewed energy. In this finale of a transcendent experience, we soaked up more of the gorgeous world we were drifting through.

At the end of the day, after the vessel returned and docked, we all hugged each other and felt blissful to have experienced the beauty of our own land and to have spent my birthday so memorably. I tell all my friends, if ever you visit Kerala, you must sail across Vembanad Lake. No words can convey the jewel tucked away in this part of India.

Our next stop was at Kochi (formerly Cochin), the port city of Kerala, where my niece Leelamma lived. Fort Kochi is the traditional colonial city which still bears the signature of many rulers in India. The Portuguese, Chinese, Dutch, British, and Arabs have left their cultural mark on it. Walk down its streets and you immediately feel the cosmopolitan air and European influence. The name Cochin, or "co-chin," means "like China." And it looked like China in the 14th century after the Chinese came here and installed Chinese nets. Even today fishermen use these nets, operated from the shore, and you can see them as you drive into Cochin.

Leelamma has a three-story colonial-type home, modernized with air-conditioned rooms. Many tourist attractions lie near her home, such as the resting place of Vasco da Gama (the voyager who opened the path for Portuguese trade and colonization in India), a Jewish synagogue, and two famous cathedrals: Santa Cruz Basilica, built in 1558 by the Portuguese, and St. Francis Church, built in 1503 and the oldest European church in India.

We spent much time exploring the streets and visiting curio shops. The fish market was interesting. It lay just minutes away from my niece's house and offered a wide variety of seafood, and people flocked to it early in the morning. Leelamma is well-versed in bargaining with the fisherman and we feasted on their catch for all the days we stayed with her.

I spent a final few days with my brother Philip in Angamally before returning to Los Angeles.

When the plane lifted off from the airport I had another look at my entrancing Kerala. Lush green vegetation and coconut palms carpeted the ground, and as the plane cut through the clouds and I lost sight of my homeland, my mind started ruminating. This was a trip to quench my nostalgia, to bring closure to my mother's death, and to see my siblings and cousins after 14 long years. This was a trip where Bina could see that Nandini was well-settled. This was a trip to show my family my birthplace and expose my children again to our wonderful heritage. This was a trip where I could stand up in my home church and thank everyone for praying for me. This was a trip where I could sit in my ancestral home for one last time to dwell about my formative years. This was the trip where I could see my own homeland with a tourist's eye and view the rapid progress of my birthplace. Usually I yearn for the next trip when I take off from an airport. This time my mind was at peace when I thought that I was going back to Los Angeles, my home now.

Chapter 28

Return to the Crucible

Life was quickening in April 2007 and things were looking normal for me. At work I was leading the launch of electronic medical records for the new hospital in the Kaiser, Panorama City campus. I had meetings to attend and many undertakings to carry out. I had to schedule training for busy physicians without disrupting their patient load. I had to review and correct all the pre-printed hospital admission orders before entering them into the software program. I had to coordinate templates for certain specialty clinics. I had to make sure that the nursing and paramedical staffs gained the skills to chart patient care electronically. I had to make programmers aware of the concerns of this project's consumers.

Unlike deployment of outpatient medical records, which took place department by department, the hospital deployment had to occur in one day with all departments coming aboard at the same time. The pharmacy and the paramedical staff were thrilled to get legible orders and information about patients at the click of a mouse rather than waiting hours for a chart. However, we faced the usual resistance to change with a new system. The bed coordinators, the admission clerks, the emergency room staff, and many managerial staff only welcomed the new technology after much education and cajoling. It was an ongoing challenge and I enjoyed every bit of it. Now, when a person was admitted to the hospital, nobody had to wait for the chart to reach the emergency room or the hospital floor to see the patient's history. Physically and emotionally I was stable and life had some meaning and hope for me.

The City of Hope held a yearly reunion for the transplant survivors. I had done a routine follow-up CT scan the day before and was awaiting the results. As Bina and I were driving to the event, she was stroking my right cheek to show her pleasure that we could attend such a gathering to meet other patients who had faced similar threats.

Suddenly she stopped and asked, "Can you turn the other cheek toward me?"

I said, "I'm driving," and added jokingly, "Do I have to do everything the Bible says?"

"Show me the other cheek," she persisted. She said she felt there was a rough spot on my right cheek.

I said it was a thickened muscle as I had been clenching my jaw. But with me, as with any cancer survivor, recurrence was a fear that dangled in the mind all the time. I felt a lightning jolt and suspicion started rising.

Ever since my cancer diagnosis, I had gone to my surgeon friend Dr. Ashok Reddy whenever I had a medical problem. This time he felt my cheek and said I had a lump the size of a marble and it needed a biopsy.

The next day I had a needle biopsy and it showed that my cancer had recurred. The CT scan and PET scan revealed an additional tumor in my abdomen.

Life had thrown me back in the crucible.

I was devastated. Physically I felt reasonably well, but my mind started revisiting all my troubles from treatment so far and I was quavering inside about the next steps to take. My oncologist Dr. Nathan started me on a new medication called Revlimid. And just as a plane makes an emergency landing wherever it may be after a bomb threat, our family stopped all activities and clustered at once to plan for my next level of treatment.

I emailed Dr. Falk, my transplant physician, about my condition. When he asked if I had any siblings, I knew I was heading for a matched donor stem cell transplant. My last procedure used my own stem cells (an "autologous transplant"). Dr. Falk was considering a donor's stem cells (an "allogeneic" transplant) for me. While waiting for the response to Revlimid, he said, he would search the national bone marrow data bank for a donor with HLA-matching marrow. HLAs or "human leukocyte antigens" are protein markers found on cells in the body. He explained how the immune system uses these markers like ID cards to recognize which cells belong in your body and which don't. A close match between your HLA markers and your donor's can reduce the risk that your immune system will attack your donor's cells or, conversely, that your donor's cells will attack your body.

He also reminded me how close matches promote engraftment. Engraftment occurs when the donated stem cells start to grow and make new blood cells. It also reduces the risk of the post-transplant complication called graft-versus-host disease (GVHD). GVHD occurs when the immune cells from the donor attack the host (your body).

Dr. Falk said brothers and sisters have a better chance for a close match. I sent word to my siblings, and they were ready to do anything to help. The City of Hope had arranged for tissue typing for them. My brother Philip flew in from India, my older brother George came from Oman, and my younger sister Molly arrived from Michigan. It was a poignant family reunion at a time when my emotions were at their lowest. We talked into late hours of the night, recalling stories from our childhood days. We reminisced about our parents. I felt a warm fondness rising in the midst of my uncertainty because of this family get-together.

But the City of Hope informed us that none of my siblings were a match for me.

And since I was an Asian male in the West, the probability was low that I would get a perfect match from the bone marrow data bank. But the transplant co-coordinator kept searching it exhaustively.

I went to a Bible study group at my church on Saturday evening. That group had been praying for me ever since I learned about the recurrence. One Saturday the leader of the study group, Jane Kasel, anointed me with oil and swabbed it gently over the tumor on my face. The group laid hands on me and prayed fervently. We had a prayer meeting with some of our family members and friends, and with one accord we prayed for a matching donor and a successful procedure.

My brother Philip stayed with me for a month. He was grieving over the loss of his wife, who had died of a stroke a year ago, and I had asked him to remain with me for my own moral support during the worrisome days ahead. Philip had spent most of his career in the Indian Air Force. After completing his term there, he went to Oman where my father lived and worked there till he retired. We had never had much chance to be together since he left for Air Force service at a young age, so this time was very special for both of us. Philip is a handyman. We painted the garage, fixed the plumbing, and changed electrical fixings. We talked and exercised and traveled together, and all these activities allayed some of my anxiety.

I had an appointment with Dr. Falk and I asked Philip to come along. The nurse took my vitals and led me to the doctor's room. He looked at Philip and asked, "Did you know you had another brother?" With a warm grin, he told us that they found a 32-year-old male who was a perfect match for my marrow.

Now I was at a crossroads. Bina and I sat down in his office for a long discussion about the protocol and side effects if we decided to go through with the procedure. Decision time. Decision time. I was showing some response to the Revlimid treatment, but another life-threatening stem cell transplant might or might not increase my odds of survival. If a choice involves material or status, you can tolerate a mistake. But when it comes to your life, you need exceptional clarity.

The doctors gave me one year to live after the recurrence. I thought: I have had a good life, raised a family, crossed the oceans to make a home in Los Angeles, and enjoyed a rewarding career. Did I have to endure the misery of this life-threatening treatment again on the chance that we could cure the condition? Did I have to jump into the crucible and see what would happen? Where would I find the strength to get through the long periods of agony? How much would treatment disrupt my family? What would happen to our finances? What quality of life would I have if

I survived this ordeal? What else could I do? In India many people retire at 58, and so I thought: Maybe this is God's timing for me to return to Him. Should I simply give up or should I give it a try? All these questions tormented me.

Gone are the days when your doctor or oncologist would tell you which treatment to select. The research and clinical trials seem to occur at warp speed and you get thrown into the excruciatingly complex realm of modern medical decision-making. For me, opinions among the specialists were divided. But against all odds we now had a donor, and I leaned on the thought that this was divine appointment. Perhaps we should proceed with the transplant.

I had seen a few patients who had undergone a stem cell transplant and done well, including myself. But I had never seen anyone who had had a second one. How many could you have and what was the mortality rate? What would I be like afterward, physically and mentally? How much more could I take and still trouble my family to look after me? One side of my mind said, "It is better to be ignorant and jump in," but my logical mind wanted answers. Yet were the statistics and outcome results really going to change my choice? I think only spiritual strength can give you the power to make decisions like this.

We discussed it a lot. We prayed a lot. We researched a lot. My friend, Dr. Fred Rosenfelt firmly advised me to undergo the transplant. He said it was my best chance for a complete cure. The attending physician Dr. Falk was confident I could go through the procedure, as all my major organs were fairly healthy. From childhood I had a basic motto: "If the choice is act or don't act, act." This approach had helped me make many decisions in my life and accelerated my achievement of goals that seemed unachievable. And in the end I acted here too.

We went through preliminary tests for the transplant procedures. But I still had deep doubts about the outcome. I completed critical paperwork in case I didn't make it. The estate planning was done. I drew up my last will and testament, and Bina and I had a sound understanding about the insurance and other assets we had.

I was admitted to City of Hope on September 16, 2007. The campus now had a new hospital dedicated to bone marrow transplants. It was a state-of-the-art building, with an advanced filtering system to keep infections at a minimum. The lobby was spacious, with relaxing lounge chairs and glass walls from floor to ceiling. I found that the rooms were comfortable and offered a view of the San Gabriel Mountains. The beds also acted as scales, so patients did not have to stand up for weighing. The modern bathrooms had grab bars and other safety features for frail patients. The hallways were long and wide so patients could walk around to maintain their mobility. The nursing stations were well spread out and many of the nursing staff recognized me from last time. Overall, the ambience was reassuring and very pleasant.

A table and chair stood outside my room, where Vivek and Bina could read or do office work when I was sleeping or resting. The signboard on my room said, "Biohazard and chemotherapy patient."

Then the coordinator told us that the donor stem cells had arrived by air the previous night and that the infusion would take place that afternoon. I have no memory of the actual procedure. I had asked for sedation, since I did not want to feel any discomfort or emotions.

Emotions! Yes, I was getting life-sustaining cells from another human being to replace my own, which had failed to keep the cancer away. We asked for the name of the kind-hearted person who had taken the time to donate life-giving cells to a complete stranger. The coordinator said that for privacy and security reasons they could tell us only the age and gender. It was a 32-year-old male.

Once again, the medical team marked the day of infusion on my chart as Day 0. From then on it was a countdown — or count up — to see when the marrow would graft and start producing new cells. They collected blood samples daily to monitor counts and basic body functions. I was started on a heavy dose of medications to suppress my immune system and prednisone to prevent rejection of the infused stem cells. In addition to the normal reactions to chemotherapy, now I had to face the side effects of these powerful medications.

Nausea and vomiting soon appeared, and after a few days my mouth was full of ulcers, which compounded the discomfort. My frequent, assisted visits to the bathroom were an added torture. I gained some relief with morphine drips. Nobody had to tell me to take bed rest, as I could not find the strength to get up from bed. The ceiling above me limited my visible world.

Other side effects were starting to appear. My blood pressure went up and my blood sugar rose to abnormal levels, so I needed insulin to control it. When I looked in the mirror I noticed that my eyeballs had shrunk, my eyebrows were sparse, and I had no hair anywhere on my body. My skin started turning dark and scaly rashes appeared on my forearms, legs, and back. My muscles were wasting away and struggled to hold up my body weight, and I needed more and more help every day. I thought to myself: This is how I will be when I am 85. But the reality soon set it and I told myself, "Hold on to the IV pole when you get up from bed and walk to the bathroom. Grab the safety bar when you sit on the toilet. Lean onto the wall when you take a shower and sit down on a chair when you towel yourself dry."

It was hard to accept this accelerated dysfunction, and my mind grew discouraged and started sliding into depression. I had tapes on hypnosis, classical music, and Christian devotional songs to calm me and distract me. TV and books were difficult as my eyes easily got fatigued. More than all the devices, it was the presence of Bina, Tara, or Vivek when I opened my eyes that kept me going.

At night, whenever I woke I saw Bina or Vivek sitting next to me asking what I needed. The night nurse came in regularly with feline tread to check the IV lines and add new medications. She changed the dressing of the Hickman catheter on my chest. In a soft voice she asked if I needed anything. My usual answer was: " Something to stop my nausea and help me sleep." It was a constant battle to find a comfortable position in bed and fall back to sleep. There was a clock on the wall but the time seemed to crawl.

The daytime went a little faster. Dr. Falk had retired and Dr. Kogut and Dr. Spielberger took charge of my case. I eagerly waited for their rounds and longed for comforting news. Taking a shower in the morning became a formidable task, as I had no strength to stand and use my hands, but with help I took one every day. Getting food and drinks was easy as I could order off the menu from breakfast to dinnertime. Even so, I could not meet my body's needs and had to take parenteral nutrition intravenously.

A sense of danger hovered around me constantly and I struggled to keep my hope alive and focus on little improvements. The fear of hitting the minefield of infection and bleeding was very much alive in my mind.

Six weeks into my treatment the inevitable happened. Dr. Spielberger came and told us that the blood tests showed increasing levels of cyto-megalovirus (CMV) infection. CMV is a dormant organism in the general population but in immuno-suppressed patients like me it gets active periodically. They started me on anti-viral medications but the levels kept increasing to an alarming degree. They consulted an infectious disease specialist and infused new medications and immunoglobulin into me for six weeks to bring the CMV down.

During the agonizing days in the hospital, the value of my material goods faded from memory. My only precious possessions were my wife and children. Whenever I opened my eyes I saw one of them at my bedside checking my comfort level. Tara would bring comedy movies that I had seen with her before to make me laugh. She knew how to get chai tea latte from the cafeteria with the right temperature and sweetness. She would open the fruit bowl and encourage me to eat. Vivek would bring extra snacks and sweets from the nearby restaurant, and would walk with me in the corridor, making sure I didn't lose my balance. Bina would read the Bible and daily devotional portions at my side. She would get on the Internet and read out all the e-mails that had arrived. They kept me informed about local and world news.

On many days I closed my eyes and yearned to escape to a world without pain and suffering. But when I opened them and saw the devotion and love my family had for me, I prayed to God and asked for more time with them.

Finally, I reached the day before my discharge. But suddenly Dr. Spielberger noticed new reddish rash on my back. He canceled the discharge and prescribed more medications. Just when we thought I was home!

That week I complained of chest pain. The nurse on duty came to check me. I had a very anxious demeanor and the nurse sensed that I was heading for a complication. She made me breathe oxygen and gave me nitroglycerine tablets. My oxygen saturation had dropped and she brought in the doctor on call. An EKG showed no signs of a heart attack, but a chest X-ray revealed an accumulation of fluid in my lungs. Further tests with an echocardiogram showed I had fluid around my heart as well and I was in congestive cardiac failure.

The next few days I frequented the bathroom a lot as I had to be on medications to increase my urine output. My legs were swollen and almost numb. I received many blood and platelet transfusions to keep the counts above the critical low level.

One day the technicians did a bone marrow biopsy to see how much of the new marrow had harvested. The result: My marrow was fully that of the donor. I was immensely heartened, since that was the goal of the therapy. With the first bone marrow transplant my blood counts and physical well-being had progressed steadily, but the second one took a much longer and less predictable course.

At last, after two months in the hospital, I was discharged.

CHAPTER 29

Five Months in Bed

I arrived home after this long hospital stay in a state beyond happiness, and with a feeling of achievement. Yet the first thing I noticed was my extreme weakness. Lying for weeks in a hospital bed, along with the heavy dose of steroids, had left my muscles so feeble that I needed help to walk to the bathroom. I could sit on the toilet seat but needed help to get up. To get in and out of the bathtub, I had to lift up one leg with both hands and try to hold onto the walls. It was humiliating and frustrating. A walker and special toilet seats helped relieve these problems, but it all remained a torture.

One day I felt a chest pain. Being in an ultra-watchful mode and knowing all the side effects of the chemotherapy, I worried that it might be pericarditis. Pericarditis is the inflammation of the covering of the heart. Since I had fluid around my heart, it was logical to think that as the fluid got absorbed I could suffer pericarditis.

I reached for my stethoscope and listened to my heart. This is usually not the best idea for physicians, as they cannot objectively assess abnormal sounds in their own hearts. Yet I did know exactly what to listen for in pericarditis: the textbook description of "grated leather rubbing together."

Wow! That sound was loud and clear. I was anxious and frightened.

I was hearing a grating sound in my heart, which meant I had pericarditis.

Bina heard all the commotion and came to the room. She knew about my paranoia and reminded me that we had a clinic appointment the next day.

Next day at the clinic we all had a laugh when Dr. Kogut said that I didn't have pericarditis and told Bina to keep that stethoscope away from me.

My daily routine of brushing my teeth and bathing became laborious and one day I noticed blood in the toilet. By the end of the day I had a fever of 102.

Bina drove me to the City of Hope for evaluation. Rain was pouring down and even with the windshield wiper sweeping at maximum speed, visibility was limited. The usual drive of 45 minutes took 1 hour and 35 minutes.

Bina struggled to help me on a wheelchair and hold an umbrella at the same time. Half-soaked, we reached the evaluation area of the hospital. My blood count was extremely low, and I was admitted to the facility.

For any transplant patient, the biggest enemy is GVHD (graft-versus-host-disease). As donor cells and host cells attack one another, normal growing cells get caught up in this fight and take the brunt of the battle. Skin rash is very common and easily manageable. But damage to the liver and gastro-intestinal system can be serious and it needs very close monitoring. The blood cells, especially the platelets, are also vulnerable. When the platelets get harmed, we see a low count and the red rashes called purpura. My platelet counts were low and now I had bleeding from my stomach.

They wheeled me into the room and gave me a hospital gown, and a nurse came to do a special blood test to check my clotting time. Even though I stayed in the hospital for five months, I still cannot get used to the hospital gown, which just partly covers you and makes you hold onto the edges to close it properly.

When the nurse left I changed into my lungi and polo shirt as I do at home. The skirt-like lungi is a unique nighttime garment in Kerala. I've worn lungies from my teenage days and I've never gone in for fancy pajamas even though I am now on the other side of the globe. In college we used to wear very colorful ones to show off our collections and see who had the best. Now I have mellowed in terms of color choices, but my family knows that I don't leave home without one. And my lungies are still brightly hued. I became almost a fashion item as the nursing staff and attending physician looked forward to seeing what color lungi I would wear each day!

I had stopped investigating the details of the medications I received, as I got too worked up thinking about their side effects. Bina learned much about these drugs and spoke with the attending physician if she had any concerns. I knew I was getting a heavy dose of steroids this time and I was posted for a gastroscopy to see if a single bleeding site from the stomach might explain the blood in the stool. I actually had five gastroscopies and one colonoscopy to try to find it, but there was no localized area, just capillary oozing.

Yet my hemoglobin remained critically low and I had blood transfusions almost every day for six weeks. The sight of the nurse walking in with the blood bag in her arms used to devastate me. I knew all the side effects of a blood transfusion, from the immediate ones like chills to the long-term risks of infection and liver damage. Blood transfusion is a two-edged sword. It is life-saving at critical times, but you use it only when it is absolutely necessary.

I needed over 35 units of blood on that admission. Emails went out to the colleagues from my department and many friends and acquaintances from Kaiser, Panorama City came to City of Hope to donate blood and platelets for me. To this day members of the hospital staff occasionally stop me in the corridor and tell me that they gave blood for me, even a few with whom I associated very little. Good Samaritans came to my aid and I benefited from belonging to a large, close-knit organization like Kaiser Permanente. Sethu, my dear friend of forty years, became my blood brother, donating blood and platelets for me.

The hospital days have telescoped in my memory, as they were all much the same. The morning ritual began with the nursing staff preparing me for that day's transfusion and other procedures. After noon things slowed down a bit. A housekeeper came in and wiped the floors, and I'd follow her broom in the floor and watch for missed spots. When I pointed one out, she would swing her broom clockwise to catch it. Like a kid following ants, I did that many afternoons. It may sound childish, but looking back it was those baby things — eating, sleeping, bathing, and visiting the bathroom — that slotted my day's agenda. The dietitian checked my weight every day and recommended nutritional, high-calorie items from the menu. Many days she was disappointed to see drinks left on the side table as I could not keep much down.

Physiotherapists came daily with elastic bands and bars to stretch my muscles and make me do structured exercises. The respiratory therapist focused on oral hygiene, using five different mouth rinses, and patiently watched me clean my mouth to prevent and heal ulcers. On days when I was wheezing they attached the oxygen tube and gave me breathing treatment to open up my bronchioles.

Both preparing for and undergoing the procedures were very unpleasant. Colonoscopies were the worst, as anyone can attest, and it all gets shoddier when you don't have the stomach to take the distasteful liquid for preparation and you lack the strength to make the frequent bathroom visits that follow drinking it. There were many X-rays, CT scans, and PET scans. All required that I visit the department sitting in a wheelchair, wrapped up in that skimpy hospital gown which neither covers you fully nor keeps you warm.

Sleep, sleep, sleep. That's all I did otherwise. My eyes were fatigued and when I tried to read, I would drop the book on my chest and fall asleep.

In the evening shift, the nurses had a different routine. They cleaned the Hickman catheter in my chest, refilled the IV fluids, and balanced or caught up with the fluid balance sheet. I was always restless and made sure that the night staff remembered my sleeping medications.

The days went by without the clock dictating appointments and I counted them as in Biblical times. It was evening and morning, day one. And then it was evening and morning, day two. But there was no day of rest. The routine kept me going with multiple medications, transfusions, and visits from different specialists. The days were dull but I had time for devotion; the nights were gloomy, but I had time to doze off. The mornings brought uncertain expectations, but I received hope from the attending staff; the evenings were encouraging because of friends' visits, but I felt restlessness and anxiety about the night. And the procedures made me apprehensive, but the results were never devastating.

The five-month stay in the hospital took a toll on my ability to walk. My muscles grew slender and very weak. I lost 25 pounds and my once-smooth skin had scaly scars and wrinkles. I was bald, skinny, and emaciated. When I looked in the mirror I saw nothing attractive.

But Bina, Vivek, and Tara were my cheerleaders, reassuring me that I was still precious to them. Tara used to put lotion on my hands and legs. After she rubbed the emollient in, she would look at me for acknowledgment that the skin looked better. To me it was like toad's skin.

They used to take me out to the beautiful hospital lobby to meet other patients and gaze through the floor-to-ceiling windows. We all compared notes with each other. The conversations were limited in scope, as we all had the same questions about each other's blood count and how close we were to discharge.

I found distractions in my environment. Hundreds of doves flew around the hospital at dusk. They darted up and down, and side to side, and occasionally got bullied by a bigger blackbird. They mesmerized me as if I were a child, since I had nothing else in my mind to keep me occupied and my family knows I am not much for talk just for the sake of talking. Those swooping doves kept me enthralled even though I did not have the strength to sit for very long.

Vivek used to play chess in the lobby with me. When I said that I needed to lie down, he would take me back by the longest route to give my wasting muscles more exercise.

Staying in a hospital bed for weeks and weeks gives you a small network of fellow patients and the nursing staff gets very close to you. Bina remembers all the personal details of the nurses who attended me, such as how many children each one had, what were they doing outside work, and who was going to get married.

In spite of my haggard appearance, my blood count stabilized and I was released from hospital. When I reached home I wept, as there were days when I thought I would never see my home again.

The intense rehab regimen started the next day. The first one hundred days are critical for transplant patients to prevent infection and acute rejection of the graft. I came home with many dietary restrictions and infection prevention methods like wearing masks and sanitizing my hands several times a day. But I worked at it, because nothing was more important.

Slowly, I regained my strength. I started enjoying the taste of food again. My neighbor Andy and I ventured out onto the golf course where I used a golf-cart as I was still too weak to walk the course. After the second transplant, my immune system was too compromised for me to go back to work. At first I was devastated. My vocation defined me. Ever since I had first put a stethoscope around my neck at the age of twenty, I had reveled in my profession. Now, it was as if the very core of my being had been taken away from me. I fell into a deep depression, but gradually, the love and support of my family and friends helped me redefine my new life. I read exhaustively, rested without thinking of night calls, spent time in prayer, and savored my days with my wife and children.

The coin had flipped again.

Many sympathetic people have told me that I am a good person and didn't deserve this illness. The big question everyone has is: Why do bad things happen to good people? It is one of the most difficult issues in theology. As a physician I knew the population-wide causes for cancer, but there is usually no single identifiable cause for an individual and the timing is never acceptable.

After studying the Bible and learning much theology, I still have found no answers. And even if I had discovered one, it would not have alleviated my suffering. Our human mind will never comprehend the answer to this question, only God, who is eternal and holy.

You can also flip the coin and look at a different side of the question: Why do good things happen to bad people? When we look around, we see both sides of the coin. The sun rises for evil and good, and the rain nourishes the poison ivy and the mango tree.

Faith is the essential ingredient of spirituality. There is no spiritual growth without strong belief. Many scholars agree that faith is waiting on God's time rather than our own. It is a trust that God plans our future. There are excellent definitions of faith, but my simple approach is to see the positive side in the midst of adversities, to hope for things that are not immediately visible with an assurance that our hope has substance. When life is going well, when problems don't discourage us, few people seek faith. But it is essential to weather the storms of life. Faith, hope, and prayer gave direction to my life.

I believe that God created a perfect world. Because of sin, disease, and the free will of man, we cannot expect our lives to go perfectly all the time. I live with the assurance that the ultimate answers to life's questions belong to God and we live with what is revealed to us. My faith told me to submit to God and wait on Him, to trust in the Lord and try not to rely on my own understanding.

For there is a universal voice in every religion, every country, every heart, which comes to you when all seems lost and hope has fled, when your strength feels crushed down. It is a divine voice assuring that dependence on a higher power will give you confidence to face misfortunes and accept the truth that one day we will all "cross the river of life," and a hope that the wondrous awaits us on the other shore. In the gospel of Matthew, Jesus says, "Come to me, all who are weary and heavy-laden, and I will give you rest."

Faith is patience with God. And for me God's answer to prayer came through the love and devotion of my family, access to excellent medical treatment, and the strength to fight on. God gave me the ability to accept what I had been denying. I had to brace up to believe that whatever I lost in life would not stop my destiny, and my assurance of Eternal Life.

Faith was tested but Faith sustained me.

Joseph Varughese's 60th Birthday Speech

November 14th, 2009

It's wonderful to see my family and friends all together in the same room.

Let me tell you the story about my first birthday celebration. I grew up in a family where we didn't celebrate birthdays or anniversaries. Bina and I got married in May of 1975 and moved to Christian Medical College, Vellore for my internship. We were living in the men's interns' quarters on the seventh floor of a ten-story building with no elevators. It was a tiny room with one bed, one table, one chair and a bathroom. The first year of an arranged marriage is like dating. We try to get to know each other. My hours were long with many night calls. Bina was teaching in a school close to the hospital. On many days, I saw her running down the stairs to catch the school bus as I was going upstairs to catch some sleep after a night call.

Women were not allowed in the dining room of the men's interns' quarters, so we had food brought to our room in a Tiffin carrier. Bina bought a small kerosene stove with the idea that she could warm up the food when I come home late. But she always did something with the food to make it special. Plain rice became fried rice; bland vegetables became vegetable curry. On the day of my birthday, I got up and went to the bathroom to get ready for the day. Later, when I tried to open the bathroom door, it was locked from the outside. Hmmm!!! I called Bina's name and banged the door. I started wondering,"Had I done anything wrong? Was there some marital discord that made her angry?"

I banged again with a little more intensity. No answer. I wondered, "Did I say something to upset her?" I could smell something burning. Was there an accident with the kerosene stove?

Finally the door opened. I rushed outside to check on the stove. It was off. Then Bina smiled at my panic-stricken face and pointed to the table. I saw a cake with a lighted candle and a wrapped box with ribbons on it. I turned and looked at her. She started singing "Happy Birthday."

It turned out that she had locked me up because, living in one room, she wanted time to wrap up the gift and light the candle to surprise me.

She told me to blow out the candle. After I blew out the candles, she asked, "Did you make a wish?" What! I looked at her and said, "My wish is already granted. You are with me!!!"

That was my first birthday celebration.

Since then I have not missed a single birthday — and look what she has done today. Thank you, Bina. Thank you, Vivek and Tara, for this beautiful event.

Turning 60 is a major event in many cultures. Many societies celebrate 60 because it is considered a true rebirth. In many nations, this is the age you retire and start a new life. In India it is called *shastipoorthi*. It is a numerology term in Sanskrit for completing 60 years and it has a lot of astrological significance. Before modern medicine, few people lived beyond the age of 60. This could have been literally true for me. I am here because of the Grace of God, the miracle of modern medicine, and the love and friendship from all of you. In India, the tradition is that you go on a pilgrimage to holy places after celebrating the *shastipoorthi*. By coincidence, Shalini, our friend and world traveler, has booked a trip for us to go to Jerusalem. We want your blessings and prayers for us to fulfill this dream. Our trip will be exciting as we have good companions. Nalini, Bina's childhood friend, and her husband Nicky are traveling with us on this adventure.

Thank you, Sethu, for being my closest friend all these years. What would I have done without you? He arranged everything for me to come to the United States. His wife Geetha found a house next door to them and all we had to do was to pick up the key and move in. All of you have played different roles in my life. Your friendship in good times and bad times is appreciated. When I say bad times, they were really bad times for me. You all stood by me in various capacities to support me physically and mentally. I want to say a special thank you to Dr. Nathan, Dr. Falk, and Dr. Spielberger for their extraordinary care.

Talk about care! You need extraordinary and continuous care when you are sick. The social worker at City of Hope had warned us that I may need a caretaker 24 hours a day while in the hospital for six weeks and my rehab time would be more than six months after the bone marrow transplant. She knew our family dynamics with Bina and the kids working full time. As you all know, my stay in hospital turned out to last six months and my rehab time was more than a year. I was wondering where I would get a caretaker to look after me 24 hours a day.

Not once but twice. Bina and the children braced up to the challenge and I don't have words to express the extent of their devotion and care, but many of you have witnessed it first hand.

My kids know there are no flowers, jewelry, honey, or I-love-you's in our marriage. I confess that I take many things for granted. Tara and Vivek tell me, "Dad, you are so lucky to have mom. Do something for her!" I think it is about time. I want to say to Bina in front of our family and friends, "Bina, I thank you for all the love and devotion you have shown. A dozen roses are on their way to your doorstep to show that I still have some romance in me!"

Vivek took over all the chores I did at home when I was hospitalized, starting with checking the sprinklers and putting away garbage. In the hospital I was amazed at his wisdom about sanitation and infection control. As soon as he walked in, he would start cleaning everything I touch with alcohol wipes, starting with the telephone, IV pole, bed rails, and doorknobs. He stopped all visitors and made them wear mask and gloves. One day he was half-asleep from a restless night with me when Dr. Nathan came to visit. Vivek stopped him too and told him to wear mask and gloves, only to recognize in a minute that it was my oncologist and friend. He spent sleepless nights at my bedside, watching to keep kinks out of my IV lines and tucking in my bed sheets when I rolled over. He made me walk and sit up on the bedside several times to reduce the wasting in my muscles. I was happy to see him rise to the challenge and was ready to pass on the baton. Vivek, I love you for all the care and love for me. God bless you and reward you.

Tara is my pride and joy. She kept me from going into depression, cheering me up with stories of my past and my activities with them during their childhood. She brought old home videos of our holidays and funny movies to keep me occupied. Even though I was withering away and my eyeballs were sinking, she would lean on my chest and tell me I was handsome and charming. She gave me the desire to live and she keeps me young even though I realize today that I am 60 years old. Tara, I treasure your love and God bless you.

God gave me 60 years to live. I walked most of the years. Ran some years and I had to crawl the last few to reach this landmark birthday. If God gives me more time, I want to walk, run and maybe fly. I want all of you to be my cheerleaders as you have been in the past.

Tonight is the celebration of health. Tonight is the celebration of happiness for my family and tonight is the celebration of love and friendship.

There is a beautiful verse in the Bible that I am reminded of written by King Solomon which expresses my feelings today. It goes like this. "He brought me to his banquet hall and the banner over me was LOVE." I love you all.

Thank you for sharing this evening with me. Thank you.

* * *

Though Joseph was in good health at his 60th birthday, he caught the flu the next week and it developed into pneumonia. He spent his last days in the ICU of Kaiser, Panorama City, the hospital where he had found so much happiness and fulfillment, cared for by devoted colleagues and his loving family. To the great sorrow of his family, friends, and patients, he passed away on December 31st, 2009.

Tara's Eulogy

I am Joseph Varughese's only daughter.

If you know me very well, you know that I am not one to stand in front of a group of this size and share my heart. But today is my chance to share with the people who loved Dad most, the person Joseph Varughese is to me.

My dad was a student of "Life." He loved the prospect of every new day. He ALWAYS had a plan. He'd always say to me, "What's the plan for the day?" He used his time to study and learn more to improve himself and teach those who were around him. The most faithful student that he had was me! We were more than just a father and daughter — we were buddies, the BEST of friends.

Some of Dad's favorite things:

Of course, his love of medicine.

But not too far behind was a huge love of gadgets! He always researched and then was the first to buy all the latest and greatest electronic toys. Back in July Dad had made plans for Mom, himself, and me to attend his favorite convention: CES — the Consumer Electronic Show. He would be happy to know that we are here celebrating his life and it just happens to be the weekend of the big electronic show.

On my days off from work, I mostly hung out with my dad. We would go to lunch and run errands, which included spending seven hours waiting in line for the new iPhone or going to his favorite store — Best Buy!

When he was working, one of my favorite things to do was go to see him at the hospital. I got to see who my dad was to the people he worked with every day. They would always rave about what a great physician he was and how much fun he was as a colleague. They all admired and respected him.

Later on, my visits to the hospital were because he was ill — a little different than when he was working. But the same thing was true. All the doctors and nurses would say how much they enjoyed him as a person.

For this I am very proud.

My dad was an amazing man who encouraged and supported me ALWAYS. Not many kids can say this (not even my brother), but — he never ever raised his voice to me. He spoke to me in a gentle, loving voice. He was truly a kind, gentle, patient, and loving father.

Another love that we shared was that my dad was a Big Family Man. He adored his wife, his kids, his brothers and sisters, cousins, nephews, and nieces. Truly, he enjoyed family. Often I would get confused thinking who is related to whom? Is Mom related to this person or is Dad? The reason I was confused was because Dad loved them all the same. He treated both sides of our family as if they were truly his very own.

I am exactly the same. I am the happiest when I am surrounded by my family. Having you all here means a lot to me!

I have learned so much from my dad. His dedication to his family was shown to us in so many ways. Mom and Dad's marriage has been such a strength to me. It is so much more than a traditional love story. Actually it wasn't even a love story; it was an arranged marriage. But their life together from the beginning has been complete devotion and dedication to each other. They have taught me what a True Loving Marriage is.

My dad was a man of great faith. He never preached to me. He taught me by example. One of his happiest days was when I was baptized at a beach in Ventura.

Shepherd of the Hills was his second home. He loved the services, revivals, and most of all, Jane's Saturday study group. Thank you, Pastor Shawn and Jane, for this beautiful service.

My dad was a great teacher and logical thinker. Whenever we wanted something or needed to make a decision, he would say, "Give me five reasons." So if I came to him and said, "Dad, I want to learn to play the violin," he would say, "Give me five reasons. " If I said I wanted to buy a new laptop: "Give me five reasons." When I told him I loved him (which I did a lot!), he would say, "Give me five reasons!"

Well, Dad, I have hundreds of reasons! You were a loving father, a devoted husband, and a dedicated physician. You were honest and kind, and you were truly an honorable man.

I love you, DAD. I will miss you every minute of EVERY DAY.

Acknowledgments

This book would not have been possible without the support of a number of people. We want to express our heartfelt thanks to our editor Dan McNeill of Spectrum Editorial. Through his thoughtful revisions and skillful editing, he discovered the essence of Joseph's intent while preserving his voice. He had the remarkable ability to go beyond the words on the page to the very heart of the writer. We are so grateful for his sensitivity and compassion. We are also indebted to Michele de la Menardiere who designed the book jacket and the book layout. She interpreted our vision for the cover and evoked the spirit of the book. We want to express our deep gratitude to Abraham Verghese, author of *Cutting for Stone,* for his generosity and encouragement. We thank our uncles Philip and John Thomas who guided us through the publishing process and readily shared their contacts.

Finally, we remember Joseph, beloved husband and devoted father. He revealed his soul to us through his vivid and poignant narrative, and left us this priceless legacy of his deepest thoughts. He is our beacon – in life and death.

–The Varughese Family